PRAISE

THE
Health
CATALYST

"Dr. Avanti Kumar-Singh has been an instrumental part of expanding my knowledge of Ayurveda and is an indelible resource for those who want to heal and live a vibrant life."

—*Gwyneth Paltrow*, Founder of Goop

"Dr. Kumar-Singh is an essential leader of Ayurveda and a powerful voice in wellness. Her book is a wonderful tool to regain your vitality and understand how to apply the ancient wisdom of Ayurveda to really work for your life."

—*Tara Stiles*, Founder of Strata Yoga

"Perhaps one of the most important statements put forth and explained by Dr. Avanti Kumar-Singh in her book, *The Health Catalyst*, is 'The ability to listen to what we need is something we all are born with.' And thus, self-healing is your birthright. Here, Dr. Kumar-Singh offers a beginner-friendly introduction to Ayurveda, presenting health-supporting concepts in both accessible and easy-to-apply methods. By emphasizing the knowledge of the gunas or observable qualities within nature—both externally and internally—the author helps the reader think more dimensionally about their lived experience: not what to think, but how to think . . . and then ultimately, how to heal."

—*Dr. Pratima Raichur*, Doctor of Ayurvedic and Naturopathic Medicine

HOW TO **HARNESS** THE **POWER** OF
AYURVEDA
TO **SELF-HEAL** AND
ACHIEVE OPTIMAL WELLNESS

THE
Health
CATALYST

AVANTI KUMAR-SINGH, MD

THE HEALTH CATALYST:
How to harness the power of Ayurveda
to self-heal and achieve optimal wellness.

Second Edition

Published by Mandala Tree Press
www.mandalatreepress.com

Paperback ISBN: 9781954801400
Hardcover with Dust Jacket ISBN: 9781954801424
Case Laminate Hardcover ISBN: 9781954801417
eBook ISBN: 9781954801431

First edition August 2020

OCC011000 BODY, MIND & SPIRIT / Healing / General
MED004000 MEDICAL / Alternative & Complementary Medicine
HEA025000 HEALTH & FITNESS / Yoga

www.avantikumarsingh.com

For orders or inquiries, please use the form on the website.

To Mummy, Papa & Anjali
You gave me my wings.

To Kanwar, Zayn & Isha
You taught me how to fly.

To my students & patients
You inspired me to soar higher.

and

To Babaji
You reminded me why I'm here.

CONTENTS

Part 4: You Can Heal Yourself

Second Edition

AUTHOR'S NOTE

When I set out to write this book 4 years ago, I did so with the intention of offering a simple solution, a "prescription" for self-healing and transformation using the power of Ayurveda. Everywhere I went— whether a keynote at a medical conference, a workshop for a corporate wellness program, or a lecture for medical students and residents—I was asked the same question: "Do you have a book with all of this information?"

Eventually, after many years of hearing this, I finally sat down to write. Little did I know that when I turned in my manuscript in February of 2020, the book I had intended as a manual for self-healing with Ayurveda would become a manual for boosting immunity, decreasing anxiety, increasing energy . . . for staying healthy in the midst of the greatest health crisis and challenge of our time. Living in the new reality of a world changed by the global pandemic of COVID-19, we have been challenged in every realm of life. No doubt there will be many more new experiences and challenges ahead, and at the core of everything will remain our health.

I believe that the information in this book—based on two decades of my study and training in Western medicine, Ayurveda, and yoga therapy, work with patients and students, and personal experience—is more important than ever. I believe that what you are holding in your hands is a playbook to help you navigate the challenges that lie ahead. It is a tool to help you feel empowered in a world filled with so much uncertainty. It is a reminder to listen to the whispers coming from within . . . to write your own prescription for health in modern life, using the healing power of the ancient medicine of Ayurveda.

As I wrote in my original introduction, "If you're ready to make small changes in your daily life that will have a big impact on your health, then take my hand and let me guide the way."

Avanti Kumar-Singh, MD

Avanti Kumar-Singh, MD
Chicago
February 2022

AVANTI KUMAR SINGH

Introduction

THE HEALTH CATALYST

Ayurveda is a health catalyst. Like a catalyst in a chemical reaction, it will increase the rate of healing to transform your health and, ultimately, your life.

I know this because it has transformed my life and the lives of many of my patients, students, family, and friends. As each of them has practiced the simple habits of Ayurveda, they have felt better. They have had improved digestion, more restful sleep, and increased energy. They have felt less anxious. Their relationships with others have changed in positive ways. They have begun to experience glimpses of optimal wellness. They have begun self-healing and living more vibrant lives.

When I began my self-study and practice of Ayurveda 15 years ago, I had no idea how much it would change me. At that time, I was somehow managing a career in medicine, two young children, an equally successful husband, and a close-knit extended South Asian family. Most people would say that I "had it all," but I didn't feel that way. Instead, I felt exhausted—my body was sick, my mind was overwhelmed, and my spirit was depleted. I was in constant motion, moving from one task to another and shifting between the roles of mother, wife, daughter, physician, and countless others every day. The only time I wasn't in motion was when I was sleeping, which wasn't often.

My body kept giving me small clues to slow down and rest: a headache here, a back spasm there, constipation, weight gain, skin rashes . . . the list went on. But I kept ignoring the clues. I would put a band-aid on my symptoms and just *keep going*. Until one day I couldn't keep going anymore. I was bending over to fold a blanket and fell to my knees. I threw out my back and couldn't move for 5 days. My body had said "no more," and just like that, I was forced to slow down. Actually, I was forced to stop completely.

In my bed over the next 5 days, I couldn't do anything except be with myself. I had to ask myself some difficult questions. Questions that I didn't have answers to. Questions I would continue to ask myself for the next few months. Questions that eventually led to my leaving Western medicine and embarking upon a journey that brought me back to Ayurveda, the medicine I had grown up with.

When I turned to Ayurveda, I had no idea that this ancient healing tradition from India, the birthplace of my parents and countless genera- tions before them, would end up being the medicine that I had hoped to practice when I began medical school . . . and the medicine that would heal me. I learned how to live in harmony with nature, how to adjust my daily habits and routines to support my health, how to tune in to my inner wisdom and access the healing power within me. I learned how to slow down and be still, how to be kind to myself, and how to focus on what really mattered. Ayurveda changed me and changed my view on everything. It changed how I live my life and it changed how I practice the art of medicine.

Ayurveda can be intimidating for many people because it is often presented in a complicated way that makes it difficult to understand and even more difficult to apply to one's life. I always hear patients who come to my office and students who come to my lectures apologiz- ing that they don't do yoga or that they don't meditate, as if to imply that yoga and meditation are prerequisites for Ayurveda. Let me assure you, you do not need to know anything about Eastern medicine, yoga, or meditation to begin incorporating the principles and remedies of Ayurveda into your life. You only need an open mind and a willingness to try something unfamiliar.

What follows is a "prescription" for self-healing and transformation, based on my many years of study and training in Western medicine, Ayurveda, and yoga therapy; my personal journey; and my work with hundreds of patients and students. The solution I offer is simple. My goal is to meet you where you are and make this powerful healing tradi- tion accessible to you—to present the ancient medicine of Ayurveda as a health catalyst to achieve optimal wellness in modern life.

2

If you're ready to make small changes in your daily life that will have a big impact on your health, then take my hand and let me guide the way.

Avanti Kumar-Singh, MD
Chicago
October 2019

AVANTI KUMAR SINGH

I had to ask myself some difficult questions.

PART 1

My Journey Back to Health

"Physician, heal thyself."

—*Luke 4:23*

Chapter 1

STARING AT THE CEILING

I remember that night like it was yesterday, yet it was almost 20 years ago. I'd been on a string of night shifts, probably four or five in a row, and it was the last one before I had a few days off. It was about two o'clock in the morning, and the emergency room staff, myself included, was waiting for the next round of ambulances to roll in. I thought maybe I could take a couple minutes to rest. So I found an empty space—not exactly a room because there weren't any walls in this ER—and drew the curtain closed. I made sure the bed was locked in place before lying down on top of the fresh white sheets. I made a mental note to strip the bed when I was done—my white coat wasn't really white anymore. Its faded brown stains were probably red bloodstains three or four washes ago. Underneath my coat, I wore a wrinkled gray T-shirt and light-blue hospital scrubs that I had taken out of the dryer when they were still damp.

When my head hit the pillow, I closed my eyes tightly, hoping that when I opened them again, I'd be in my bed at home and realize this was all a dream. And . . . that didn't happen. I opened my eyes and glanced around the room. There was the sink and the counter with random supplies still in sterile packing, there was the movable tray table and the extra chair for a family member, and there above my head and slightly out of my visual field was the vital signs monitor, blinking and waiting for the next patient to be connected to it. I was still in the emergency room. It had been about two minutes since I closed my eyes.

I took a deep breath as I stared at the ceiling tiles, which I can remember vividly. They were those square Styrofoam tiles with a white metal frame holding them in place. One minute I was counting the ceiling tiles, and the next my thoughts shifted to counting the number of patients I had already seen during my shift. And I had to stop often because I kept losing my place. But what was most aggravating was that when I was trying to count my patients, I couldn't remember their names, their faces, or what they had come in for. I couldn't remember what care they had received in the ER and whether I had discharged them or sent them up to the floors in the hospital. I couldn't remember . . . anything.

Tears started gently rolling down the sides of my face into my ears. Then came the gasps for air when sadness knocked the wind out of me. I turned onto my side and curled into a ball, trying to stifle my crying. It was distressing for me to not recall the faces of my patients. It's one thing to not remember a patient's name or what complaint they came in with, what their history was, or even what they left with—that can all become a jumbled mess after seeing a dozen or more patients during a shift. But to not remember anyone's face? I searched my mind and still couldn't remember what any of them looked like even though I had just seen them in the previous 6 hours. It was at that moment, staring at the ceiling, that I realized something had to change.

The next evening, I went out to dinner with my husband, Kanwar. I met Kanwar a year before I applied to medical school, so he had been with me through all of my training and knew what becoming a doctor meant to me. We were sitting in an Italian restaurant, catching up because we hadn't seen each other all week. I was working the night shift and he was a rising associate at a major law firm in Chicago, working long hours late into the evening, so when he got home, I was already gone to the ER. We started talking about this and that and then I said to him, "I'm leaving." His face fell, and I realized he thought I meant something else. I quickly corrected myself and said, "No, No, No . . . I'm leaving emergency medicine."

For the next few moments, which felt like hours, we sat there in silence—a silence I thought might swallow me whole. And then Kanwar said, "Are you feeling okay? What's going on?"

I nervously laughed at his questions and then said, "What's going on is that I can't do this anymore. I can't practice this kind of medicine—the kind of medicine in which I can't remember the faces of my patients just a few hours after seeing them." I went on to tell him what had happened the night before on my shift. The tears started again.

Twenty years later, I still remember the mixture of emotions I felt sitting there in the restaurant with Kanwar—the deep sadness mixed with crippling shame that I was somehow weak and couldn't really hack it. That not remembering my patients' faces meant something about me as a doctor and as a human being. We spent the rest of dinner talking about my decision, and I ultimately decided not to walk away. Not yet.

Staring at the ceiling that night in the emergency room set into motion a period of deep self-reflection about why I had become a doctor and what being a doctor meant to me. It made me ask myself some difficult questions I had avoided most of my life because I had a singular focus: to become a doctor. To have the letters "MD" after my name.

A period of deep self-reflection.

Chapter 2

LIVING THE IMMIGRANT DREAM

I always knew I wanted to go to medical school. At least, that's the way I remember it. I realize now that what I actually wanted was to be in a profession that allowed me to help other people. To my 10-year-old self, helping people meant being a doctor. As a first-generation South Asian girl growing up in the 1980s in a south suburb of Chicago, the list of "what to be when you grow up" was (1) doctor, (2) doctor, and (3) doctor. There's no doubt that I was heavily influenced from a young age by my parents to think about medical school.

My father came to the United States in 1968 to pursue his postgraduate studies in biochemistry at Columbia University. He was the eldest of three children, and it was his parents' dream for him to come to the United States. Back then, it was a very, very big deal to come to the United States to receive higher education. It was a badge of honor not only for you but also for your entire family. It implied that you were intelligent and signified that you were destined for great success in life. When my father received his acceptance to Columbia, he knew it wasn't just because he was intelligent; he knew it was because he was one of the lucky ones who had just received a ticket to a better life.

A few months after arriving in New York, my father went back to India and married my mother. They had a traditional "arranged marriage," which meant they were introduced because someone in my father's family knew another family, who knew another family, who knew someone in my mother's family. What's funny about this story is that when my father went back to India to meet my mother, he didn't actually meet her. His parents handed him a photograph with the expectation that he would approve of moving forward. Then his whole family, which included his

11

parents as well as his younger brother and sister, went to meet my mother first—without him. It was only after they approved of her that they took my father with them for the second meeting. If you ask my mother about the second meeting, she'll laugh and say that at first, she didn't raise her eyes to actually look at my father. It was only after the elders had "decided" that she finally looked at him. They were married on January 5, 1969, and a few days later, they immigrated to the United States from India. My mother boarded an airplane for the first time, dressed in an ornate pink sari and a simple brown wool coat that had two pockets filled with a few things she couldn't fit into her suitcase: a pair of shoes and her dreams for the future.

The stories my parents tell about their early days in Brooklyn are some of the most beautiful stories I've heard. They recall the simplicity of that time and the adventure of it all. They lived in a small, one-bedroom apartment in a brownstone walk-up on Ocean Parkway in Brooklyn, New York. My mother remembers to this day—50 years later—every detail of that apartment: the few pieces of furniture they had, the mismatched set of dishes, the color of the walls and the carpet, and the view out the front window of people walking on the sidewalk and cars driving on the parkway.

As my parents settled into life in America, they met other couples who had also immigrated from India a few months or even a few years before them. My father fondly recalls being welcomed into their homes and into their hearts. It was with these friends that they took weekend adventures to upstate New York and into Manhattan. It was with these friends that they learned where to shop for ingredients similar to those they used at home in India—staples such as long-grain rice, lentils, wheat flour, and spices. It was with these friends that my mother bought her first pair of snow boots because she was now living in New York in the middle of January and only owned flats and open-toed sandals. Those friends became their new family in their new home away from home.

I was born 2 years after my parents got married, and 18 months later, my younger sister, Anjali, was born. My father then got an opportunity at a prestigious lab in Chicago, where I've lived ever since. I grew up in a small, tight-knit family in a south suburb of Chicago called Flossmoor. It was a mostly white, middle-class community with one of the best public high schools in the state, while also being affordable and only 40 minutes from the city, making it an obvious choice for highly educated immigrants who wanted the best education they could get for their children. My sister and I still joke that by time we entered high school, our classes looked just like the United Nations because so many of our classmates' parents had the same idea as ours and had moved to our suburb

My parents quickly developed a close circle of friends—other Indian families who had all come to America with the same dream of creating a better life than what they had left behind in India. These families quickly became my extended family. Like all families, we had our share of friendly competition and arguments. We grieved together and we celebrated together. We literally did everything together. Every weekend, we would gather at someone's home and our mothers would cook and talk and our fathers would play cards. All the kids would be down in the basement playing and creating mischief. We didn't know it at the time, but we were sharing the everyday moments of our lives that would end up mattering the most to us in the future.

When we were growing up, my parents would talk to me and my sister about the importance of being independent, of always being able to stand on our own two feet to support ourselves—to never have to depend on anyone. They instilled in us a disciplined work ethic and the belief that we could do anything and be anything. And so, at 10 years old, I decided I would become a doctor—not just because my parents had planted the idea in my head, but also because I had so many examples around me. Many of my "aunties" (what we called Indian mothers who weren't our actual mothers) were physicians. They had come from India in the 1960s when the United States opened its doors to welcome foreign medical students to complete their postgraduate training and residencies in the United States. I quickly figured out that becoming a doctor was a way to help other people and that it was also a very respected profession for a woman to pursue. And so I dreamed of the day that I could wear a white coat similar to those I had seen my aunties wearing—but embroidered with the letters "MD" after *my* name instead.

When I entered high school, I still had my heart set on becoming a doctor. From the very beginning of the first semester of freshman year, I made sure I took every requirement I needed to apply to college and declare that I wanted to be pre-med. That became my singular focus—to kick ass in every subject and be at the top of my graduating class so I could apply to the most prestigious universities in the country. However, this was never pushed upon me or my sister by my parents. They were the exception to the stereotypical Indian parents who helicoptered around their kids, monitoring their every move. Instead, my parents had this gentle way of encouraging us to find the strength and the will within us, to work hard and always to do the best that we could. They had an unwavering belief in us—that we were intelligent enough and capable enough to achieve anything we wanted. Anything.

So I worked hard in high school. I was among the top 15 in a graduating class of 600 students. I attended the University of Chicago, entering as a premed, biology major and graduating as a premed, art history major because I figured it was the only time in my life I would study something other than science. After college, I took a year off because, again, I figured it was the only time in my life I would be able to experience something other than medicine. I considered the Peace Corps, but that was a 2-year commitment. I also considered teaching, but only committing for a year didn't feel right. In the end, I worked at Cook County, the public hospital in Chicago, running a large grant in health education, and took that year to apply to medical school.

Even during that year off, I never considered choosing a different profession. I had chosen my path and never wavered from the idea that I was going to be a doctor. Looking back now, I wish I had questioned whether Western medicine truly was the kind of medicine that I wanted to practice, but I didn't. I made the assumption that Western medicine was my path and that Western medicine had all the answers to help people heal.

Admittedly, this doesn't quite make sense because I grew up in a South Asian household in which the principles and practices of Ayurveda, the traditional healing science of India, were a part of my daily life. It was just the way we did things. I never stopped to consider where those traditions came from. I knew that those traditions, those ways of eating and living and healing, came from my family's country of origin and that my parents were doing what they knew. But I never stopped to think about the fact that the way I had lived for the first 18 years of my life might be an alternative to Western medicine. Perhaps it was because my father encouraged me to pursue a scientific method of healing. Perhaps it was because my mother encouraged me to complete the highest education I could. Or perhaps it was because I knew the sacrifices my parents had made to come to this country. I felt a sense of responsibility to achieve the dreams that they had brought with them from India, the dream of having a better life and the dream of educating their two daughters to receive the highest degrees possible. And so I applied to medical school. A year later, I was admitted to Rush Medical College. I was living the immigrant dream.

Chapter 3

FIRST HEAL THYSELF

There are two phrases, words of wisdom, I have carried with me for most of my adult life. The first is "First, do no harm."[1] This phrase is part of the pledge that I took during my "white coat ceremony" when I started medical school and one that I carried with me throughout my medical training. It's a phrase that kept my ego in check because it was a constant reminder to never overestimate my ability to help a patient heal and to never underestimate my ability to cause a patient harm. It's a phrase that always reminded me of my duty as a physician to my patients.

The second phrase is "Physician, heal thyself."[2] This phrase is one that I read when I was doing research for my undergraduate senior thesis in art history on the art of medicine and one that I carried with me from college. It made an impression, and so I filed it in the back of my mind and didn't think about it for many years . . . and then I got sick.

Looking back, I realize I started to get sick in medical school. There was the slow weight gain, the occasional headaches, and the constipation that was an annoyance I didn't need in my busy life. I attributed it all to stress. And to fatigue. But like my classmates around me, I ignored the symptoms I was feeling and pushed through . . . because training to become a doctor wasn't an easy path. I knew that when I signed up for it.

Training to become a doctor was rigorous. It was taxing. It was exhausting. And it had always been like that. The hours we put in—going

1. Hippocrates, *Of the Epidemics*
2. Luke 4:23

to classes and labs, studying, and then working in the hospital—were expected because those who went before us had studied and worked the same long hours. If they could do it, you had to do it too. To them, it was a rite of passage. To me, it felt like hazing. Almost every single day, I had to psych myself up and tell myself that I could hack it, that I could survive, and that it would all be worth it in the end because becoming a doctor was so important to me.

When I started my residency in emergency medicine, I always seemed to throw out my back after a week of continuous shifts and just before I had a day off. It was almost as if my body was waiting until I had 24 hours off before it would give me a lesson to learn. But I never learned, and I never listened. I would pop lots of Ibuprofen and put a Band-Aid on my symptoms. I'd figure out how to cope with the pain and get right back onto the treadmill of long hours in the hospital. This pattern continued for years. Every time I would throw out my back, the pain would get worse. I would rest for a day, I would take more Ibuprofen, and I would go back to work.

By the time I finished training, I had gained 25 pounds. The headaches had increased in frequency and severity. The constipation had become a daily problem. I developed plantar fasciitis in both of my feet because I was standing so much and was carrying a lot of extra weight on my body. Every single day, the pain I felt just walking around was excruciating. My solution was to get another pair of clogs with another pair of custom orthotic inserts so that I could just . . . keep . . . going. And then it happened. My body finally said, "No more."

A few months after the night shift when I had stared up at the ceiling, telling myself something had to change, I threw out my back. It was the smallest movement. I wasn't lifting anything. I wasn't carrying anything. I was simply bending over to fold a blanket at home. The next thing I knew, I was on the floor doubled over because I was in so much pain.

I spent the next 5 days in my bed, unable to move, unable to do anything. I was forced to rest, sleep, take pain medication, and do nothing, so I had a lot of time with myself. A lot of time to ask myself a lot of questions—and to actually answer them. They were the questions I had started asking myself that night after staring at the ceiling in the emergency room. "Why did I decide to become a doctor? What does it mean to me? Am I practicing the kind of medicine I had hoped to practice when I started medical school? Is this all worth it? Is being a doctor and working

My body finally said, "No more."

as a doctor more important than my own health?" There I was, day after day, working in the emergency room trying to help patients get better while I was getting sicker and sicker. The irony of this didn't escape me then and doesn't escape me to this day.

When I finally recovered from throwing out my back, I left Western medicine. I simply walked away. I had to because I was getting sicker every day. Every day, I felt more pain, not just physically, but also mentally and emotionally. My spirit was slowly withering away. I didn't know who I was anymore. I knew I had to do something to save myself before I could help anyone else. And the phrase that I had tucked away so many years before while doing my thesis research in college came rushing back: "Physician, heal thyself."

I spent the next few months trying to figure out what to do next, how to get better. I tried to figure out where and how I had lost my health. I was only 32 years old and I was sicker than my grandfather was when he died at 89. How had he done that? How had he stayed so vibrant and healthy that he never took any medication and never had a medical issue until he broke his hip during his morning walk at the age of 88—just 1 year before he died? How had I, his eldest grandchild, a physician, lost my own health while learning to take care of others' health?

I remembered how I used to watch my grandfather, who I affectionately called "Babaji," pray every morning when he would come to visit us in the United States. He would wake up at the crack of dawn, drink some water, use the toilet, take a bath, and then sit wrapped in a towel in front of his altar. He would do a breath practice, meditate, and then pray. After that, he would get dressed, eat breakfast with his chai, and head outside for a morning walk. That was his morning routine. His routines continued throughout the day. He ate his meals at the same time, only ate foods that were fresh and in season, and never ate leftovers. I remember when we would go to visit him in India during our winter vacations and I would ask him for my favorite dishes because I loved Indian food. Sometimes he would say yes and sometimes he would say no, and if he said no he would explain why. "No Avanti, you cannot have yogurt in winter, it is too cold." or "*Beta* [my child], make sure you add ghee to your dahl because it will make you feel warmer." I used to giggle and smile. I went along with what

Babaji said and never asked a lot of questions because I figured it was just the way you were supposed to eat when it was cold outside in India.

As the months passed after I threw out my back, Babaji started appearing in my dreams at night. I could feel his presence with me all the time and had this sense that he was gently nudging me in a different direction to find the answers I was looking for. Then I heard the whispers coming from within: "Go back to your roots." I needed to go back to what I had learned when I was growing up. I needed to go back to the way we ate, the way we kept our home, the self-care practices we were taught. I needed to go back to the way we lived and the things we did that I never paid attention to—all the things that were just a part of my daily life. I needed to go back to all the things I had abandoned when I left home so I could fulfill my dream to become a doctor.

And at that moment, those two phrases, the words of wisdom that I carried with me for most of my adult life, became my guide. "Physician, first heal thyself and then do no harm."

Chapter 4

WHAT I DIDN'T LEARN
IN MEDICAL SCHOOL

I learned a lot in medical school. I spent 4 very long years learning everything about the human body. I dissected a cadaver and learned what every layer of tissue was, where every organ was, where every vessel was and where every nerve was. I marked them, memorized them, and then named them during exam after exam.

I learned how the human body works correctly by studying anatomy and physiology. Then I learned how the human body works incorrectly and what to do about it by studying pathology, pathophysiology, microbiology, and pharmacology. I learned how to listen to patients and ask them about their symptoms. I learned how to palpate and percuss and perform a physical exam. I learned how to put all those symptoms and physical findings into a differential diagnosis and then learned which tests to run, which medications to prescribe, and which consultations to request.

Yes. I learned a lot in medical school. I learned so much that, years later, when I was working in the emergency room, I couldn't figure out why I felt as if I hadn't learned anything in medical school. I couldn't figure out why I felt like I wasn't really helping any of my patients. Because it seemed that the same patients were coming in again and again and again . . . with the same symptoms, worsening symptoms, and additional symptoms. It was a pattern that never changed.

What was really going on here? Was I missing something? Was there something medical school and my training hadn't taught me? It didn't seem like the three-step process we had learned to help our patients heal was working: the "name it, blame it, tame it" approach. First, identify where the problem was based on the anatomy, physiology, pathology, pathophysiology, and microbiology. Then identify what the problem was based on the history, physical exam, labs, and imaging. Finally, identify how to eliminate the problem based on the treatment options available. Clearly, the approach of providing a cure, of eliminating the symptoms in our patients, was not working.

This question of "Am I missing something?" never left my mind. Years later, when I left Western medicine, I began to dig deeper. I needed to find out what I was missing because I had spent most of my adult life up until that point with a singular focus—to help people heal—and I wasn't succeeding. I started by asking myself more questions. "Are there gaps in my knowledge? Is there something they didn't teach me in medical school? Is there something I didn't learn well enough in medical school? Are my clinical skills lacking? Am I not asking patients the right questions? Am I not listening well?"

In addition to all the information we studied in the classroom and memorized from books, we also learned clinical skills. We needed to know how to communicate with patients and how to examine them. We spent a lot of time learning to ask patients questions about the what, how, how long, when, and where of their symptoms. We learned to ask about their own medical history and their family medical history. We were taught to ask open questions that allowed the patient to describe things in their own words, instead of leading questions that might suggest a specific answer. We were taught to listen carefully to what patients said so that we could figure out what to ask next.

I remember being in my clinical skills classes, practicing with my classmates, trying to learn how to ask open questions and then how to listen so I could ask more questions. It was always this delicate balance between figuring out what the next question was and, at the same time, not leading the patient to a specific diagnosis of what I thought was going on. As the years went by, I became more proficient in these skills—asking questions, listening, determining the next question, and eventually getting all the information I needed from a patient to figure out how to help them. But here's the thing I realized: I wasn't really helping them. Although I could create a differential diagnosis, order the appropriate tests, and then base my treatment recommendations on all of this information, I wasn't helping my patients heal—I was just providing temporary relief of their symptoms.

Heal, not just relief from symptoms

The question of "Am I missing something?" remained. I began a journey to discover what helps people heal. After studying healing systems from many cultures and traditions, I received advanced training in Ayurveda, the healing system of my family's country of origin and the tradition I had grown up in. After I began to study Ayurveda, I realized what I was missing. I was missing the mark on the listening part. I was listening in a way that wasn't really serving my patients to the fullest. I had been listening with two main objectives. The first objective was to listen for the specifics—the what, how, how long, when, and where of the symptoms. The second objective was to listen for the sequence so I could put the patient's symptoms into the timeline of their life and the events that led to them showing up in my exam room. I needed to change how I was listening. Actually, I needed to relearn how to listen.

It wasn't enough to just understand the story of the symptoms. I had to go beyond the story and understand the impact the symptoms had on the patient in every area of their life. I needed to listen to the clues about how the symptoms affected their relationships with others, their work, their interests, and their everyday life. And then I needed to ask more questions based on what I heard. I needed to ask questions about their sleep habits, dietary habits, work habits, and other daily habits. I needed to ask them about their dreams, their hopes, and their wants for the future.

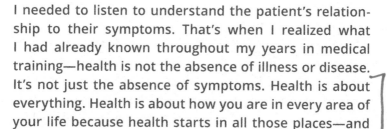

I needed to listen to understand the patient's relationship to their symptoms. That's when I realized what I had already known throughout my years in medical training—health is not the absence of illness or disease. It's not just the absence of symptoms. Health is about everything. Health is about how you are in every area of your life because health starts in all those places—and health is also lost in all those places.

In Western medicine, we were trained to believe that health is the absence of symptoms and the absence of illness. We were trained to believe that our role as physicians was to get rid of the symptoms—to cure our patients. But what I learned from traditional systems of medicine, from Ayurveda, is that health is not about curing.

> Instead, health is about healing or transforming your relationship to your symptoms—examining the meaning you attach to your symptoms, changing how you view them, and then making changes from the inside out.

As I immersed myself in the study of Ayurveda, I began to recognize the kind of medicine I had wanted to practice when I started medical school so many years ago. Ayurveda changed everything for me. Ayurveda changed how I saw myself. Ayurveda changed how I interacted with everyone around me. Ayurveda changed the way I viewed the world. Ayurveda changed how I practiced the art of medicine.

Case Study[3]

Kelly was a 25-year-old woman who had been experiencing increasing stomach pain after eating anything. For the past 10 years, she had been going to specialists and getting tests that always came back without a definite diagnosis. She had tried to manage her symptoms with various elimination diets, and each time she'd get some relief for a few weeks and then the pain would return.

During our second session together, we were talking about toxins, toxic load, and the digestive fire. I was leading her through a toxic load inventory in which I asked her detailed questions related to the five main factors that contribute to toxic load: lifestyle/routines, diet, environment, relationships, and work. When we got to the questions about her environment, specifically about her home and space, she said it was stressful because even though she had her own apartment, she hadn't really spent any time there. She told me that, although she had lived there for over a year, she still hadn't decorated it, her fridge was always empty, and there was always garbage to take out or laundry to do. When I asked her more

---

3. Name and identifying details have been changed to protect the privacy of this individual.

about this, she said that the reason that this was happening was because she was spending five to six nights of the week either at her mother's house a few miles away, or at her boyfriend's apartment in the city. I began to dig a little deeper, and she went on to tell me that always going from place to place created feelings of anxiety and instability. She felt ungrounded and even unsafe at times.

She then told me that her parents had divorced when she was a teenager and that they had joint custody, so she was constantly going from one house to the other. We talked more about her stomach pain and she told me that when she was younger, every time she had the pain, she would end up staying at whichever parent's home she was at that week for a few days longer. At that moment, I saw Kelly's "lightbulb moment." She had uncovered her relationship to her symptom of stomach pain. It was the way that she felt more safety and security because when she had pain, she could stay put and didn't have to be constantly moving from one parent to the other. Her pain was showing up then, and had continued to show up now, to make her stop moving around and feel safe and secure. Together, we came up with a plan that she would draw a line in the sand and have a discussion with both her mother and her boyfriend and tell them that if they wanted to see her, they needed to start coming to her apartment.

When Kelly came back for her third session a month later, she told me that her stomach pain had decreased dramatically. She said that she had talked with both her mother and her boyfriend and that for the last month, she had been spending five nights of the week in her own apartment. She had decorated her space and cleaned it up, she had food in the fridge and had even bought a few plants. She felt safe, secure, stable, and grounded. Her pain hadn't gone away completely, but she had transformed her relationship with her pain. She had asked her pain what it was trying to tell her. And then she had listened.

What is the pain trying to tell you.
LISTEN!

Chapter 5

THE HEALER LIES WITHIN

When I had the realization that health is about transforming your relationship to your symptoms, I knew I had to relearn how to listen not just to my patients but also to myself. I started thinking about my children and how I was always telling them what to do, expecting them to listen to me. "Yes. No. Don't touch that. Do this. Don't do that." I was teaching them to listen to me, their mom, because I was keeping them safe. I was also teaching them to listen to someone outside of themselves. I wasn't teaching them that trusting themselves and listening to their internal wisdom was also important and ultimately would be the most important voice to listen to when they grew up. There it was. The truth. If, as children, we weren't taught to listen to the whispers that came from within, then how could we possibly know how to listen when we became adults? That's what happened to me, and that's what happened to my patients.

We spend the first part of our lives learning how to listen to others and forgetting how to listen to ourselves. We play in groups to share and take turns. We work in groups to collaborate. We create groups to fit in. Unless we're taught otherwise, we believe that the way we are with others is the only way to be—share, take turns, collaborate, fit in . . . listen to others. We forget that we must also develop how we are with ourselves, that we must nurture our ability to hear and listen to our internal voices. No wonder patients have forgotten to pay attention to their inner wisdom and listen to their inner voice. They are too busy listening to others in the hope that someone, anyone, can help relieve their suffering.

All through my training, I routinely ignored the voice within that was whispering to me. Instead, I'd consider a differential diagnosis of my symptoms and then go to other residents and ask for their opinions. I would look for the answers in my textbooks and from my peers and mentors. I was always looking for the answers outside of myself. The irony is that I had the answers within me all along.

There is a "universal truth" I learned when I studied traditional healing systems throughout the world: our thoughts about our symptoms ultimately determine our course of healing. Our symptoms cause us to think thoughts, which then evoke feelings that cause our action or inaction, which ultimately determines the course of our healing—which can lead either to illness or to health. (See image 5.1.)

My symptoms during my medical training—the plantar fasciitis and weight gain and constipation and headaches and chronic back spasms—were all speaking to me, but I wasn't listening. It wasn't until these symptoms stopped me, quite literally, that I finally started to hear what they were telling me. Lying there in my bed, in pain and unable to do anything, I had a lot of time to think. I realized that my physical symptoms created feelings of inadequacy within me . . . feelings that perhaps I wasn't strong enough to be a doctor. Those feelings caused my inaction of ignoring the pain to prove I was capable enough to be a doctor and ignoring my internal voice that was telling me to slow down. My inaction had determined my course of healing, which led to illness rather than health. I realized that my physical pain was nothing compared to my emotional, mental, and spiritual pain. My body was exhausted, but more importantly, my mind was scattered, my emotions were disturbed, and my spirit was depleted. I had lost my connection to myself.

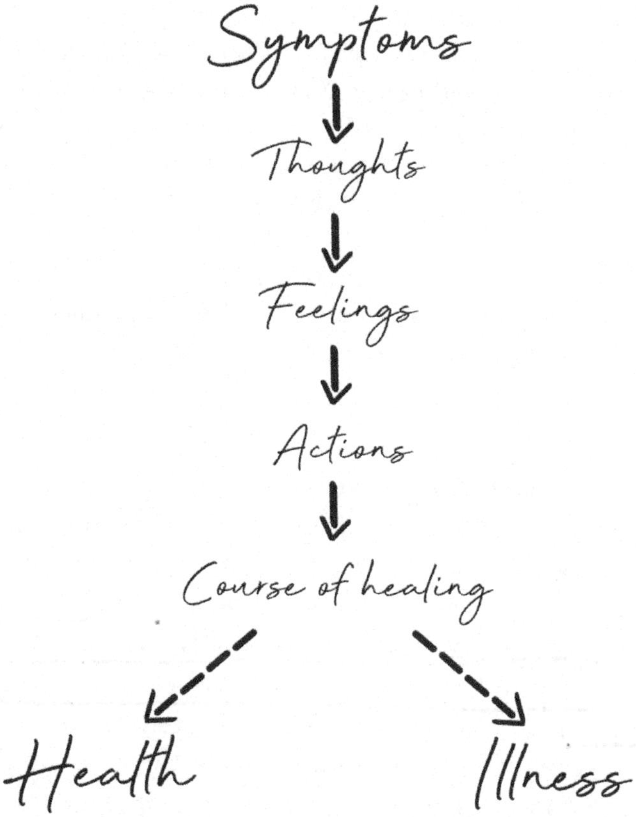

Symptoms
↓
Thoughts
↓
Feelings
↓
Actions
↓
Course of healing

Health   Illness

Image 5.1 Thoughts Determine the Course of Healing

And then something shifted. In the quiet, alone in my bed, the whispers got louder. I could finally hear what my heart—my higher self—was saying. My head was able to translate those whispers from my heart to what I knew from my past experiences and my years of studying and training. The connection between my heart and my head was once again created, and my inner wisdom had a way to speak to me again. When I finally understood that healing was about transforming my relationship to my symptoms, I started to listen to myself again. I would say, "Okay, symptom, you're showing up. You're here. What are you here to teach me? What is out of balance within me? What do I need to do now to learn from you and to relieve you?" As I transformed my relationship to my symptoms, I suffered less and I began to heal. When I finally listened to the whispers, everything changed. (See image 5.2.)

After 20 years of studying and training in Western medicine and in Ayurveda, here's what I know:

If you are suffering, you have two choices. You can ignore the whispers, or you can listen to them. If you ignore them, they'll eventually become louder and louder until you can't ignore them anymore. However, if you get quiet and listen carefully, you'll realize that the whispers are coming from you and that your inner voice is telling you something. When you go inward and listen to the voice within—when the connection between the head (intelligence/knowledge/past experiences) and the heart (inner wisdom/higher knowing) is made—that is when thoughts, feelings, and actions shift. That is when healing begins. That is when you realize that the real healer lies within.

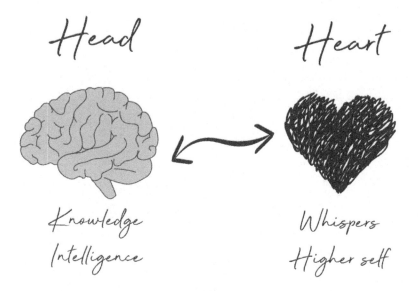

Image 5.2 Inner Wisdom

Chapter 6

FINDING INNER MEDICINE

When I left Western medicine, I thought I was leaving it for good. I was sick and tired of being sick and tired and of not being able to really help my patients who were sick and tired. And let me be clear—I didn't believe that Western medicine was hurting me, or my patients for that matter. I just didn't believe that Western medicine was helping me or my patients as much as I thought it should. I felt something was missing. Little did I know that what was missing had been right in front of me all along.

Like many others, I started looking for answers at a time when I desperately needed my health. Being sick and tired wasn't an option anymore because I had two young children to care for at home. Because I didn't know what else to do, I did what I knew—I returned to the ways of my childhood, the time of my life when I had been healthy. I returned to the way we ate and the way we lived. I returned to Ayurveda. And slowly, day by day, week by week, and month by month, my health improved. As my health improved, my curiosity reemerged . . . what was Western medicine missing?

I spent the next few years immersed in self-study of various healing traditions from around the world. I met teachers and guides who practiced a range of traditions, including Ayurveda, traditional Asian medicine, shamanism, and pranic energy healing. I learned about the rich history and healing methods of these systems. I used the herbal remedies and plant medicines of these systems. Over time, I found what was missing in Western medicine—the connection of the patient to their inner knowing of what healing and health are.

I realized that Ayurveda was the medicine that I had wanted to practice when I started my training in Western medicine. It was a system that looked at the whole person connected to everything rather than a person connected only to symptoms. It was a system that centered on the individual, not the illness. And it was part of a universal, collective truth that is found within. What I had been looking for had been in front of me all along. Ayurveda, the medicine of my ancestors, was the system of "inner medicine" in which the key was the healer within.

Ayurveda is connection.

Connection to what is outside of you:
You ← → Nature

If I asked you what nature is, you'd probably tell me that nature is the sun and the moon, plants and trees, lakes and oceans, and animals and insects. And you're correct, nature is all of these things. But what if I said that we, human beings, are also nature? In Ayurveda, nature is everything outside of us and also *is* us. We are one with all of nature at the most fundamental level because we're made of the same raw materials—the five elements in different combinations—space, air, fire, water and earth. (See image 6.1.)

In other words, we as human beings are a microcosm of the macrocosm of nature.

When we connect to nature, we are actually connecting to the pulse, or resonance, of the Earth, which was discovered by physicist W. Schumann in 1952. The Schumann resonance, a frequency of 7.83 hertz, is the exact same frequency as alpha waves emitted from the human brain. In alpha state, we are more relaxed and our physiology becomes balanced. Conversely, decreased time in alpha state causes imbalance, stress, and anxiety, which then weaken the immune system. This link between the Earth's "pulse" and humans was further proven in a study by R. Wever 20 years later. Wever looked at what happened when subjects were housed in an underground bunker for 4 weeks and blocked from receiving the Earth's natural frequency of 7.83 hertz. Over time, they developed

[handwritten margin note: Nature is everything outside of us and also is us.]

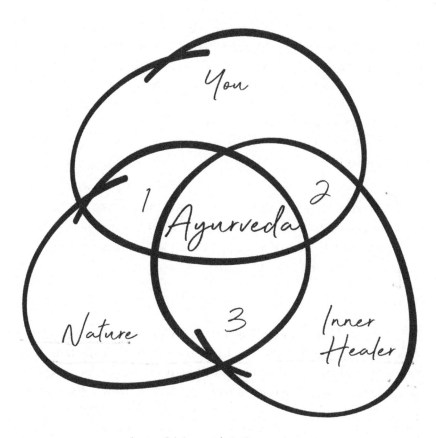

Image 6.1 Ayurveda Is Connection

headaches and became emotionally distressed. However, the symptoms lifted when Wever added the Schumann frequency back into the environment through a manmade transmitter tuned to 7.83 hertz.[4] In essence, when we are connected to the pulse of nature, we support our health.

Unfortunately, many of us have lost our connection to nature and, as a result, have lost our health. We go to work early in the morning when it's still dark outside and leave work late at night when it's dark again, quite literally never seeing the light of day. We eat strawberries and blueberries in the cold winter by freezing them in the summer. We eat mangoes that don't grow where we live by having them flown into our grocery stores from places where they do. We cook with microwave ovens and consume food that is in boxes and wrappers to save time on cooking and eating. We climb artificial stairs and walk on moving belts for exercise. And the list goes on and on.

> Our days have been designed around technology and convenience that was meant to improve our lives but instead has destroyed our health. All because we have lost our connection to nature.

One of the keys to healing with Ayurveda is maintaining our connection to nature and living in harmony with nature's rhythms. These are daily and seasonal rhythms created by the movement of the earth in relation to the sun—rhythms of nature created by nature. When we rise, sleep, eat, play, and work in harmony with the light of day, the dark of night, and the change of seasons, we are connected to what is outside of us—the sun and the moon, plants and trees, lakes and oceans, animals and insects . . . all of nature.

---

4. Wever, R. (1973). Human circadian rhythms under the influence of weak electric fields and the different aspects of these studies. *International Journal of Biometeorology, 17,* 227. https://doi.org/10.1007/BF01804614

Connection to what is inside of you:
You ← → Inner healer.

inner healer = gut instinct / higher self / soul

THE VOICE WITH THAT KNOWS WHAT WE NEED FOR HEALING TO OCCUR

In many cultures, there is a belief that there is a universal intelligence that resides within each of us—a limitless source of information that we can access anywhere and anytime. This universal intelligence is also known as "gut instinct," "higher self," or "soul." In Ayurveda, this universal intelligence is the "inner healer," the voice within that knows what we need for healing to occur. When we get quiet and listen, we are connected to the inner healer that can access this limitless source of information. (See image 6.1.)

This "higher self" has the answer long before the analytical brain does—and there is research to prove it. In one study, subjects were asked to play a card game in which the goal was to win the most money. The subjects were given two stacks of cards to choose from, one that was rigged to give big wins followed by big losses and one that was rigged to give small wins and almost no losses. It took about 50 cards before the subjects had a feeling of which card stack was "safer," and it took about 80 cards before they could explain the difference between the card stacks. More significantly, however, the subjects' palms began to sweat before drawing from the riskier card stack after only 10 cards. In other words, the subjects showed anxiety responses long before their conscious mind was aware of the danger. Their "higher self" was guiding them toward safety from the start.[5]

However, many of us have lost our connection and, as a result, we suffer more. Most of us think this universal intelligence is outside of us. So we send our requests for guidance through dreams, wishes, and prayers. We give our power to others we think will have the answers. We put our faith in doctors we hope will "fix us" and decrease our suffering. We ignore the whispers coming from within and slowly lose our ability to hear our inner voice. As a result, we slowly lose our health.

When we learn to connect with and listen to our inner voice, we understand what we really need. Then we can seek out information and guides that can help us. This is how we can access the universal intelligence, the healer within, that already has the answers.

---

5. Bechara, A., et al. (1997). Deciding advantageously before knowing the advantageous strategy. *Science,275*(5304), 1293–95. https://doi.org/10.1126/science.275.5304.1293

Connection between what is outside and inside of you:
Nature ← → Inner healer.

Every day, our senses take in thousands of inputs from nature. The sights we see, the sounds we hear, and the things we smell, taste, and feel are all sensory inputs from nature. These sensory inputs are created by the time of day, the weather, the season, the planets, the land, animals . . . and other human beings. Every single one of these sensory inputs affects us in some way, creating a reaction of some kind—biochemical, physiological, physical, mental, emotional, behavioral, or spiritual. When we realize that everything outside of us creates a reaction inside of us, we have a new understanding of health that can transform our relationship to our symptoms. (See image 6.1.)

However, most of us avoid the reactions within us that are created by sensory inputs outside of us. We ignore and fail to process the reactions created in our bodies, minds, emotions, and spirits, and then we can't understand why we suffer. We can't understand why we are having headaches or pain or insomnia or anxiety or depression. We can't understand why we have symptoms, illness, and disease.

According to Ayurveda, everything in our life affects our health because everything outside of us creates sensory inputs that then create reactions within us. This means that our lifestyle and routines, our environment and space, our work and interests, our relationships and our diet all create sensory inputs that then create reactions within us that then affect our health. The key is to process or "digest" the reactions created within us in a way that supports our health. When we understand that the sensory inputs from outside of us are creating reactions within us, we have connected nature to the healer within—and that's when healing begins.

Case Study[6]

Julie was a 52-year-old woman who came to see me because she felt fatigued all the time. She told me that she woke up every morning feeling tired and had a hard time getting out of bed. In addition, she was experiencing constipation and frequent headaches. She had been to her Western primary care doctor, who ran blood tests which all came back "within normal ranges" and then sent her home with recommendations to eat more fiber, drink more water, and meditate daily.

---

6. Name and identifying details have been changed to protect the privacy of this individual.

As we began to talk, she told me these symptoms had developed over the past 2 years and the severity and frequency had progressed rapidly over the past few months. As I explored further with her, she told me that she had recently divorced her husband after 22 years of marriage, sold their family home, moved to a one-bedroom apartment in the city, and was working as a consultant to support herself. She described how her relationship with her ex-husband had spiraled downward with daily arguments—and she didn't tell anyone because she was ashamed that she couldn't make her marriage last. Julie realized that her constipation, headaches, and overwhelming fatigue were the result of unprocessed and undigested emotions of anger, shame, sadness, and fear. When she understood that what was happening outside of her—in her relationship with her ex-husband—was creating reactions within her that she was not processing or "digesting," her understanding of her symptoms shifted.

Ayurveda is individual.

In Western medicine, we talk about quantitative measurements—labs, tests, and images. We focus on how much, how many, and what size. There are "normal ranges" for everything and people are fitted into this construct of how they measure up to the "norm." One of the most important aspects of Ayurveda is that it is a qualitative science in which one size does *not* fit all.

The qualities of symptoms provide experiential information about the relationship we have to our symptoms, which, in turn, determines our course of healing and maintenance of health.

This is a huge perspective change for most of us from Western medicine, in which health is measured by comparison to "normal ranges" of diagnostic tests and the degree of illness is measured by abnormalities seen in numbers and on images.

In Ayurveda, we discuss the qualities of symptoms and of everything in nature. These qualities are not black and white, but instead have many shades of gray. Instead of using measurements, in Ayurveda we describe symptoms according to how we experience them, how they feel and behave. After all, that's how we connect with symptoms. When we have a fever, we say "I feel hot and sweaty," not "My body temperature is above the normal range of 97.0 to 98.6 degrees Fahrenheit." When we have a skin rash (infection), we say, "My skin is red, swollen, and warm," not "My white blood cell count is increased." The qualitative feelings of symptoms, not the quantitative data, influence our experience and understanding of illness and health. And the experience each of us has of a specific symptom is personal.

In Western medicine there is a differential diagnosis for every symptom or set of symptoms that we fit the patient into. When we treat only the symptom, we provide some initial relief to the patient, but we don't provide healing for the patient. In Ayurveda, we consider the symptom and then we focus on the individual person. We look at the patient from a 360-degree perspective to examine every aspect of their life to start to identify the root causes of the symptoms, because in Ayurveda, symptoms show up a few months to a few years to even a few decades after the initial cause of imbalance in the human system. In Ayurveda, we treat the individual person, not just the symptom.

Ayurveda is within you.

Perhaps the most interesting thing about Ayurveda is that it's something we already have access to inside of us. It's always amazing to see the progression of students and patients as they move from understanding to knowing and finally arriving at the realization that Ayurveda is already within them.

When they first learn about Ayurveda, they say that it's logical and "just makes sense." Intellectually, their brain understands the concepts. For example, the Golden Principle in Ayurveda, which says that "like increases like and opposites reduce," makes sense. It's logical that if you add hot to hot, it will get hotter and, alternatively, if you add cold to hot, then it will decrease the hot.

As my students and patients continue learning Ayurveda, they say they already know the principles intuitively—and they know the principles "feel right." The idea of living in rhythm with the seasons makes intuitive sense. When it's cold outside in winter, we should conserve heat

"LIKE INCREASES LIKE & OPPOSITES REDUCE."

to stay warm and dress warmly and eat warm foods. Or, when it's hot in the summer, we should do things to cool off and stay indoors during the hottest times of the day, eat cooling fruits and vegetables, and dress in lighter fabrics. We intuitively know that adjusting our clothing, diet, and lifestyle during different seasons supports health.

After living Ayurveda, I am confident that you, like my students and patients, will arrive at the realization that Ayurveda is a universal, collective truth that has been passed down for thousands of years and is part of our essential essence and humanity. Throughout history, humans have always found a way to live with their environment to survive. They built shelter for protection from the weather and knew to go indoors to stay warm when it was cold outside or sit in the shade for protection from the heat of the sun.

What was true thousands of years ago is still true today. What is true on the other side of the world on a different continent, in a different country, is also true here on this side of the world on this continent and in this country.

The wisdom in this medicine, in Ayurveda, is a universal, collective truth that has always been true, is true now, and will continue to be true in the future. Modern medicine didn't get us here; inner medicine from the wisdom of the collective did—which is Ayurveda.

PART 2

Ayurveda 101

"Every human being is the author of
his own health or disease."

—*Buddha*

Chapter 7

WHAT IS OPTIMAL HEALTH?

[handwritten annotations: BEING ESTABLISHED IN SELF / BEING AT EASE (IN MIND / BODY & SPIRIT / THE 3 PARTS OF SELF]

The essence of Ayurveda, "the science of life," is that we are not separate from nature—we are a microcosm of the macrocosm. It's considered the oldest system of healing, over 5,000 years old, and was first recorded in India in the Vedic texts in 3000 BCE. Because it contains the roots of many other healing systems, including traditional Chinese medicine and Western medicine, Ayurveda is considered the "mother of all healing."

This is a book about self-healing, so let's start by answering the question "What is health?" According to Ayurveda, health is "being established in self" or being at ease in body, mind, and spirit—the three parts of the self.

[handwritten annotation: HEALTH = BODY SENSES EMOTIONS MIND SOUL BALANCED]

More specifically, health is a state in which the body, senses, emotions, mind, and soul are balanced. This balance, or "optimal health," is created by decreasing toxins and increasing energy in the human system.

It's important to pause and define what toxins are and how toxic load is created according to Ayurveda. Toxins are anything the human system does not need, and toxic load is created when these toxins accumulate because of incomplete or improper digestion and processing. At the same time, the flow of vital energy is increased because things that block energy are removed when toxins are removed.

The key here is that it's not about avoiding exposure to harmful substances, but rather it's about digesting and processing everything that comes into the human system—keeping what is needed and getting rid of the rest. The reality is, you can't put yourself in a bubble and eliminate your exposure to toxins, but you can decrease the accumulation of toxins, which, in turn, contributes to optimal health. In other words, if you decrease the toxic load (*ama*) and increase the flow of vital energy (*prana*), you will have increased strength, immunity, and longevity (*ojas*)—or optimal health. (See image 7.1.)

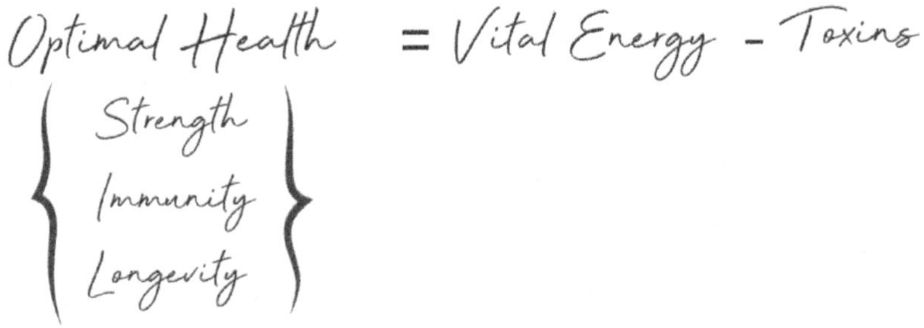

$$\text{Optimal Health} = \text{Vital Energy} - \text{Toxins}$$

$$\left\{ \begin{array}{l} \text{Strength} \\ \text{Immunity} \\ \text{Longevity} \end{array} \right\}$$

Image 7.1 Optimal Health

The symptoms I experienced during my medical training—the plantar fasciitis, weight gain, constipation, headaches, and chronic back spasms—were a result of toxin accumulation. The toxins were coming from every aspect of my life—my lifestyle, routines, diet, relationships, environment . . . and my career in medicine. Because I wasn't digesting and wasn't eliminating the toxins, they kept accumulating until they manifested as symptoms. Using the principles and remedies of Ayurveda, I started by making one small adjustment to my daily routine: I got into bed by 10:30 p.m. whenever possible to help my body's internal elimination processes that occurred overnight. I then adjusted my diet and made sure I ate my meals at regular times to help strengthen my digestion. And, finally, I committed to a daily practice of just 5 minutes of meditation and 3 minutes of breath work to increase the flow of vital energy through my system. When I rediscovered Ayurveda, the healing system I had grown up with, I learned how to decrease my toxic load and how to increase my vital energy. I experienced ease in my body, mind, and spirit. I became reestablished in myself and reacquainted with my inner wisdom. Ayurveda was the catalyst I needed to transform my relationship to my symptoms, take control of my healing, and restore my health.

Chapter 8

THE ROAD FROM
HEALTH TO ILLNESS

According to Ayurveda, all of nature is a unique combination of the five elements (*mahabhutas*)—space, air, fire, water, and earth. When we live in harmony with nature and these five elements, we have optimal and vibrant health. When we don't live in harmony with nature, we progress from toxin overload to symptoms to illness and, finally, to chronic disease. In Ayurveda, the road from health to illness is not a straight one but instead a progression through six stages that lie on a continuum. Health and illness are not black and white constructs in Ayurveda but instead have many shades of gray. (See images 8.1 and 8.2.)

Stage 1: Accumulation

The first stage of illness is accumulation. This is when an imbalance, caused by *not* living in harmony with nature, begins to accumulate. At this stage, there are usually no symptoms. For example, in the winter months, continuing to work long hours without regard for nature's rhythm of decreased daylight that encourages more rest, reflection, and relaxation indoors is an example of not living in harmony with nature. This can lead to decreased immunity. The increased exposure to viruses in the winter then creates a higher chance they will get into the body via the nasal passages and begin to accumulate, but there are not any symptoms.

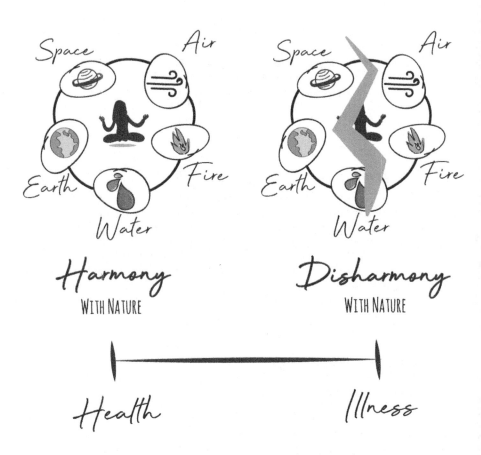

Image 8.1 Harmony with Nature

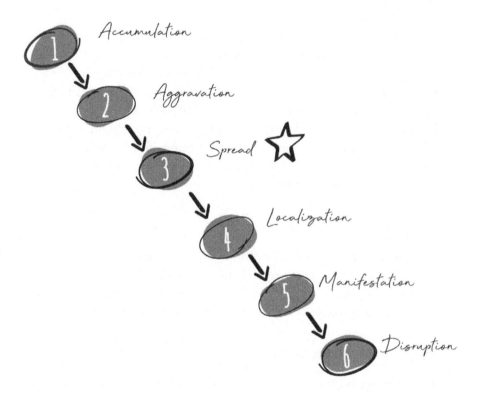

Image 8.2 Six Stages of Illness

Stage 2: Aggravation

The second stage is aggravation. This is when the imbalance starts to spill over wherever it's accumulating. Symptoms still don't appear, but there is some aggravation to the normal state. Continuing with the example above, if there is an imbalance caused by viruses in the nasal cavity, it will spill over into the lungs, but no symptoms will appear.

Stage 3: Spread

The third stage is spread. This is when the imbalance has overwhelmed the place it is accumulating in the body or the mind and starts to look for other places in the human system to accumulate, creating low-grade, nonspecific symptoms. Complaints of "not feeling well" or "not feeling right" are common. This stage is the critical point in the disease process, because you either course-correct or you begin to suffer. In my example, the virus overwhelms the nasal cavity and begins to accumulate in the lungs, producing low-grade malaise, a feeling of decreased energy and nonspecific "stuffiness" of the nose.

Stage 4: Localization

The fourth stage is localization. This is when the imbalance finds a new area of weakness where toxins have also accumulated and more specific symptoms begin to appear. Continuing with my example, symptoms progress to chest congestion, cough, and fever, producing the flu.

Stage 5: Manifestation

The fifth stage is manifestation. This is when normal function is compromised in the area of weakness and full-blown symptoms are present. In my example, pneumonia would manifest with difficulty breathing, productive cough with chest pain, fever, and weakness throughout the body.

Stage 6: Disruption

The sixth stage is disruption. This is when there is dysfunction embedded in the area of the weakness and the human system can't reverse the damage. The dysfunction can also spread or become chronic at this stage. Continuing with my example, respiratory distress can progress to fluid accumulation around the lungs (pleural effusion) or in the lungs (lung abscess).

So, the road from health to illness starts with the buildup of toxins. When the toxins overwhelm the human system, symptoms appear. These can be low-grade, nonspecific symptoms such as "not feeling well" or "not feeling right" or more specific symptoms such as anxiety, depression, GI distress, weight gain, headaches, sinus congestion, joint pain, and on and on. At this point, if we course-correct and begin to decrease the toxic load, we can avoid progression to symptoms, illness, and chronic disease. (See image 8.3.)

Image 8.3 The Road to Disease

Ultimately, the journey in Ayurveda is the daily practice of course correction between toxin elimination, which creates health, and toxin accumulation, which creates illness.

Chapter 9

YOU ARE WHAT YOU DIGEST

We've all heard the saying "You are what you eat." And it's not completely true. Yes, the quality and types of foods you put into your body matters. But if you're only focusing on the foods you're eating, you're missing an important piece. This is why so many people fall short of their expectations of feeling better and having more energy on an organic, whole foods diet. There's more to the story. Your digestive fire is a key to your health.

According to Ayurveda, your digestive fire (*agni*) is critical for optimal health. A strong digestive fire will take anything that comes into the system, absorb, extract, and keep the nourishing parts it needs, and burn off or eliminate the rest. A weak digestive fire will not be able to keep up with this process, and thus toxins (*ama*) build up, overwhelm the system, and create imbalance, which then leads to symptoms, and can result in illness and chronic disease.

We must process and digest thousands of sensory and energetic inputs all day long and keep what is needed and eliminate the rest. Unprocessed food, experiences, and emotions build up as toxins. Once the toxic load overwhelms the system, symptoms show up. Our body's internal digestive fire or metabolism is the main way we absorb what we need and eliminate what we don't. (See image 9.1.)

You are not what you eat; you are what you digest.

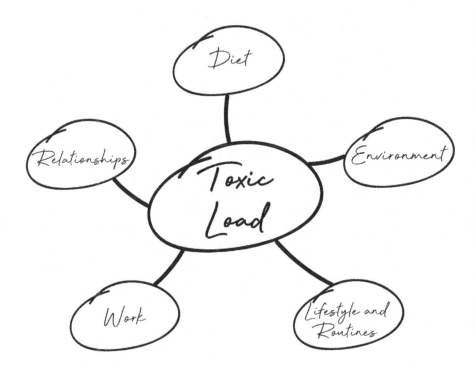

Image 9.1 Toxic Load

The piece most people miss is that it's not just about food. The reason so many people don't feel better just by changing the foods in their diet is that the mouth is just one gate of entry into the human system. There are many other gates of entry—the five senses, and thousands more at the energetic level that we cannot consciously perceive.

Digestion is about our ability to process all aspects of life—food and drink, experiences, memories, and sensory impressions.

The body and mind are exposed to hundreds of things to process every day. They take in sensory inputs through all five of the senses—eyes, ears, nose, mouth, and skin—which then create reactions within the human system. These reactions are biochemical, physiological, physical, mental, emotional, behavioral, or spiritual.

If we keep everything, regardless of whether it is health-supporting or health-weakening, we have toxin accumulation, and, at some point, the toxic load overwhelms the human system to begin the mentioned six stages of illness.

For example, I remember driving my car on a warm and sunny morning with my windows open, listening to music and enjoying my commute to work. The next thing I knew, I saw a bicycle messenger get hit by a car. In that moment, I had a sensory input through my eyes and another through my ears because my window was open and I heard the "thump" of the bicyclist crashing into the car. Those sensory inputs created reactions within me—an emotional reaction that triggered a memory of falling off a bike and injuring myself and a physical reaction that caused my body to tense up and my breathing to become rapid.

At that point I had two choices. I could either digest and process the reactions that I was having, or I could choose to push them down and repress them. By calling a friend and feeling the emotions fully, I digested and processed the reactions—I kept what I needed and eliminated the rest. If I had repressed my reactions, I would have added to the toxic load within me. And if I continued to repress my reactions, eventually it would have led to toxin accumulation, which would then create symptoms, illness, and chronic disease.

This is where the concept of toxic load really becomes important. Anything that we don't digest, that we don't process, eventually builds up and creates a toxic load within us. Toxic load comes from many different places, not just diet and the environment, which we have become very focused on over the past decade. According to Ayurveda, there are five areas that contribute to toxic load, which most of my patients and students had never considered before. Toxic load is created by lifestyle and routines, diet, space and environment, work and interests, and relationships. Toxic load comes from everything in your life.

Chapter 10

THE DANCE OF BALANCE

Let's go back to the idea that according to Ayurveda, health comes from living in harmony with nature. But how do we live in harmony with nature? We live in harmony with nature by tuning in to the way nature exists and respecting its intelligence. We live in harmony with nature by following its daily and seasonal rhythms. We live in harmony with nature by consuming the bounty it creates for us. And when we live in harmony with nature, we ensure the continual flow of life force energy (*prana*), which creates optimal health and vitality. (See image 10.1.)

$$\text{Optimal Health} \begin{Bmatrix} \text{Strength} \\ \text{Immunity} \\ \text{Longevity} \end{Bmatrix} = \text{Vital Energy} - \text{Toxins}$$

Image 10.1 Optimal Health

In the context of Ayurveda, harmony with nature creates balance of the composition of the five elements within the human system at any moment. However, this "elemental composition" is constantly changing—there is a constant dance between balance and imbalance. When thinking about the dance between balance and imbalance, it's helpful to think about the idea of "nature vs. nurture." Nature (*prakruti*), our genetic blueprint, is the unique ratio of the five elements determined at conception and is an expression of our physical, mental, emotional, and energetic states in balance, which creates optimal and vibrant health. Nurture (*vikruti*), our acquired influences, is imbalance, however subtle or gross, which creates symptoms, which then leads to illness, which then leads to chronic disease. (See image 10.2.)

As you can see from the image, this dance between balance and imbalance, nature versus nurture, is not static. It's always in flux, always moving back and forth. Therefore, the ratio of the five elements changes every day, even hour to hour. This means that depending on the balance or imbalance of our "elemental composition," we will have different experiences. In balance, we will experience vitality. Out of balance, we will experience symptoms. And the experience each of us has of a specific symptom is personal and individual.

Balance ⟵ ⟶ Imbalance
Nature   Nurture

- GENETIC 'BLUEPRINT'
- UNIQUE RATIO OF THE 5 ELEMENTS DETERMINED AT CONCEPTION
- EXPRESSION OF PHYSICAL, MENTAL, EMOTIONAL, AND ENERGETIC COMPOSITION IN BALANCE
- STATE OF OPTIMAL AND VIBRANT HEALTH

- IMBALANCE, HOWEVER SUBLTE OR GROSS
- SYMPTOMS ... WHICH LEAD TO ILLNESS... WHICH LEAD TO CHRONIC DISEASE

Image 10.2 Nature vs. Nurture

Chapter 11

QUALITIES MATTER

As I discussed in part 1, Ayurveda is a qualitative science in which qualities matter. These qualities describe and characterize the five elements and therefore everything in nature. These qualities also describe and characterize human beings and all of the feelings, emotions, and symptoms we experience.

20 qualities in 10 pairs.

In Ayurveda, there are 20 qualities (*gunas*), which are organized into 10 pairs of opposites. These qualities are essential to understand the most important principle in Ayurveda, what I call the Golden Principle: that like increases like and opposites reduce. This principle tells us how to keep our genetic blueprint balanced and how to remedy an active imbalance that is showing up as a symptom—which I will discuss in depth in part 3. The grouping of the qualities into 10 pairs of opposites makes this principle intuitive and practical to apply. (See image 11.1.)

Having a visual image of each quality is extremely helpful when trying to identify them in the elements and then in symptoms, so let's go through a few examples.

The first two qualities, heavy/light, are simple to understand. A boulder and an elephant, which have great weight and are difficult to move, are examples of the quality of heavy. A feather, a pillow, and one sheet of paper have little weight and are examples of the quality of light.

The next pair of opposite qualities are dull/sharp. Dull is something lacking interest, excitement, or brightness, like a foggy morning, and sharp is something piercing or penetrating, like a knife.

Heavy ——— Light

Dull ——— Sharp

Hot ——— Cold

Oily ——— Dry

Smooth ——— Rough

Solid ——— Liquid

Hard ——— Soft

Stable ——— Mobile

Gross ——— Subtle

Sticky ——— Clear

Image 11.1 Ten Pairs of Opposite Qualities

Hot/cold are qualities we use commonly to describe temperature. Ice, snow, and an igloo are examples of cold, and lava, the sun, and a burning stove are examples of hot.

The next two qualities, oily/dry, are simple to picture. Things that are greasy or soapy and that bead up, such as rain on a windshield or grease, are oily. Things that lack any moisture, such as fall leaves or paper, are dry.

The fifth pair of qualities, smooth/rough, are ones we use to describe the surface of things. Things with a regular and consistent surface, such as a skating rink or satin, have the quality of smooth. Things with an irregular, inconsistent surface, such as gravel, sand, or sandpaper, have the quality of rough.

The sixth and seventh pair of qualities, solid/liquid and hard/soft, are ones we commonly use to describe the shape or state something is in. Things that are compact, firm, and with a defined shape, such as granite or wood, are solid, and things that have no defined shape and are freely moving, such as rain, are liquid. Similarly, things that are rigid, not bendable, or not breakable, such as a diamond or a tree trunk, are hard, and things that are not firm, easily moldable, and bendable, such as cotton or a blanket, are soft.

Stable/mobile are also qualities that we use frequently. Something that is fixed and not moving, such as tree roots, a house, or fence, is stable. Something that is not fixed or is moving, such as a bicycle, train, or airplane, is mobile.

The ninth and tenth pair of qualities, gross/subtle and sticky/clear, can be a little harder to visualize. Things that take up a lot of space and have considerable extent or size, such as the planets or a skyscraper, have the quality of gross, while things that are in the background or not very noticeable, such as clouds, have the quality of subtle. Things that are muddy and not transparent, such as glue or grease, are sticky. Things that are transparent, such as a window, a light bulb, or glass, are clear.

Observed qualities of elements.

As I said earlier, these qualities also describe and characterize the five elements as observed in nature. I find that when trying to understand the qualities, it's helpful to group them according to each element, because picturing each is familiar and intuitive. It's important to go beyond your logical brain that will want to prove which qualities describe each element and instead allow yourself to intuitively feel the qualities that describe each element. Let's go through each now. (See image 11.2.)

Space has the qualities of being subtle, soft, smooth, and clear. When you put your hands out in front of you, in space, how does it feel? It doesn't feel hard or heavy; it's actually difficult to describe, or subtle. However, you can probably understand intuitively how space is soft, smooth, and clear.

Air has the qualities of rough, dry, light, cold, and mobile. If you think of a windy day, the air might feel rough, dry, and cold on your skin, and it's light, which makes it mobile.

Fire has the qualities of hot, sharp, oily, and mobile. When you think of fire, you probably immediately picture something hot and sharp. To understand the oily quality of fire, think about the flames of a fire and how they flicker with an almost beading type of pattern.

Water has the qualities of liquid, mobile, oily, and soft. Of course, water is without a defined shape and moves freely. If you picture putting your hands into a bucket of water, you can likely imagine that it would feel oily and soft.

Earth has the qualities of gross, heavy, hard, solid, and stable. If you think of earth, you likely picture something that takes up space, has great weight, is firm, and doesn't move.

Now here's where you might get stuck. Don't overthink. If you over-think the qualities when you're trying to describe something, you'll start to second-guess yourself. The beauty and the brilliance of Ayurveda is that you intuitively know what qualities things have. So don't overthink it and go with your first impression. With practice and over time, you'll refine your ability to intuit these qualities without overthinking.

Hopefully going through these examples has put some images in your mind so you can refer to them when you're considering how to keep your genetic blueprint balanced and how to remedy an active imbalance that is showing up as symptoms—the felt qualities in the body and mind. The more you can understand and manipulate these qualities, the more you'll be able to describe and understand symptoms and then choose remedies for healing. Spend some time looking at various things in nature and thinking about which qualities they have. This way it will be much easier when it comes time to figure out the felt qualities of symptoms, the first step in using Ayurveda for healing.

Space

SUBTLE
SOFT
SMOOTH
CLEAR

Air

ROUGH
DRY
LIGHT
COLD
MOBILE

Fire

HOT
SHARP
OILY
MOBILE

Water

LIQUID
MOBILE
OILY
SOFT

Earth

GROSS
HEAVY
HARD
SOLID
STABLE

Image 11.2 Qualities of Elements

Ayurveda takes the five elements and combines them into three energies (doshas). (See image 11.3.) Space and air combine to create the energy of Vata, which is all about movement. Fire and water combine to create Pitta, which is the energy of transformation. And finally, Kapha is the combination of water and earth, which is the energy of structure. As you can see, each of these energies has a primary function that correlates back to the elements that combine to create it. These three doshas are how a traditional Ayurvedic practitioner (vaidya) classifies a patient to make recommendations of remedies for imbalances showing up as symptoms.

I mention this because many of my students tell me that they've done "dosha quizzes" but have no idea how to use this information. If you haven't taken a dosha quiz, please resist the temptation and don't. And if you already have taken a dosha quiz, please put away the results you got for now and don't think about them. I'm purposely presenting these concepts in a way that is more accessible and useful. I emphasize understanding qualities instead of knowing doshas, because understanding qualities is how to heal with Ayurveda. So please start with a clean slate. Start with a beginner's mind.

Symptoms are "felt" qualities.

Instead of using measurements, in Ayurveda we describe symptoms according to how we experience them, how they feel and behave. The qualitative feelings, not the quantitative data, of symptoms influence our experience and understanding of illness and health. (See image 11.4.)

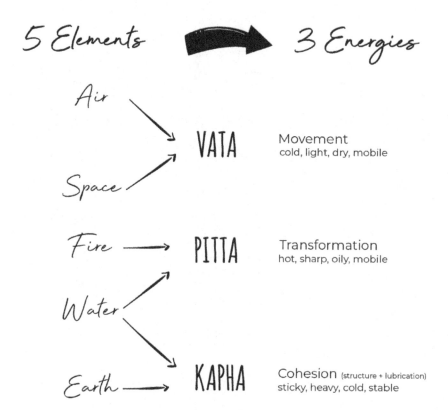

Image 11.3 Five Elements and Three Energies

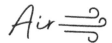 **Air**  **Fire** **Earth**

COLD, LIGHT, DRY, MOBILE

- ANXIETY, NERVOUSNESS, WORRY
- INABILITY TO HANDLE STRESS
- INSOMNIA, HYPERACTIVITY, RESTLESSNESS
- CONSTIPATION, BLOATING, GAS
- DRY SKIN, ITCHY SKIN
- UNDER-WEIGHT
- MUSCLE SPASMS, JOINT ACHES, LOW BACK PAIN
- INTOLERANCE OF COLD

HOT, SHARP, OILY, MOBILE

- ANGER, AGRESSION, IMPATIENCE
- BURN-OUT
- HEARTBURN, DIARRHEA, STOMACH ACIDITY
- ANY "ITIS" - ESPECIALLY OF THE DIGESTIVE TRACT
- RASHES, ACNE
- FEVER, EXCESS BODY HEAT, HOT FLASHES
- EXCESS PERSPIRATION
- HALITOSIS
- VISUAL PROBLEMS

STICKY, HEAVY, COLD, STABLE

- DEPRESSION, LETHARGY, APATHY
- EXCESSIVE SLEEP, FATIGUE, LOW ENERGY
- SLOW DIGESTION
- SWELLING
- UPER RESPIRATORY CONGESTION, ALLERGIES
- OVERWEIGHT

Image 11.4 Symptoms Are "Felt" Qualities

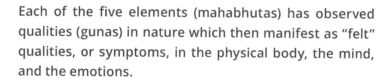

Each of the five elements (mahabhutas) has observed qualities (gunas) in nature which then manifest as "felt" qualities, or symptoms, in the physical body, the mind, and the emotions.

A simpler way to understand this is to consider the qualities of the three elements that predominate—air, fire, and earth—and then identify symptoms that share those qualities.

Symptoms that have the qualities of air are cold, light, dry, and mobile. For example, anxiety and insomnia can be described as thoughts moving across the mind, and thus have the quality of mobile. Constipation and itchy skin have the qualities of dry and cold. Rashes, acne, fever, hot flashes, heartburn, and anger can be described as heat trying to escape from the body and mind and thus have the qualities of fire—hot, sharp, oily, and mobile. Finally, obesity, swelling, congestion, and depression have the qualities of earth—sticky, heavy, cold, and stable.

Once again, don't overthink. If you overthink the "felt" qualities of a symptom, you'll start to second-guess yourself. Remember that you intuitively know what qualities things have. So don't overthink it and go with your first impression. You'll also find that you'll start to recognize these qualities when you're paying attention and living consciously—when you're listening. So once again the question is "Are you listening? Can you hear what your symptoms are telling you?" Because they're telling you some very, very important information. Your symptoms are telling you what to do to heal.

Chapter 12

THIS IS A NO-JUDGMENT ZONE

Before we start talking about self-healing with Ayurvedic remedies, it's important to realize that there is no good or bad in Ayurveda. It's what I call a "no-judgment zone." Think of things as either "health-supporting" or "health-weakening." This means that, depending on our elemental composition at any moment, our habits can sometimes be health-supporting, which will decrease toxins, and sometimes be health-weakening, which will increase toxins. The exact same habit can have either a health-supporting effect or health-weakening effect, which brings us back to the point that it's a dance of balance. In addition, what is health-supporting for one person can be health-weakening for another person. (See image 12.1.)

The idea here is that as you learn to listen to your internal voice—your inner healer—you will add things that support your health, and soon enough they'll crowd out the things that are weakening your health.

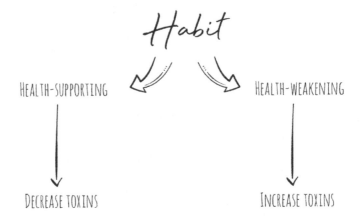

HEALTH-SUPPORTING   *Habit*   HEALTH-WEAKENING

DECREASE TOXINS   INCREASE TOXINS

Image 12.1 No-Judgment Zone

Case Study[7]

A few years ago, I had a patient named Andy, a 32-year-old man who was experiencing increasing anxiety. He told me he ate salad every day with both lunch and dinner, all year long, and no matter the season. He believed salads were "healthy" for him because he thought raw vegetables were nutrient-dense and had lots of fiber as well as countless other reasons. I told him that I thought his mostly raw diet was a significant cause of the intensifying anxiety he was experiencing. When I asked him if he enjoyed eating salads in the winter, he laughed and said, "No. I can't stand eating cold salads in the winter, but . . . " His internal voice was telling him something, but he was ignoring it because he was focused on all the health benefits of raw vegetables. Andy's internal voice was telling him that it was health-weakening for him in the winter, but he wasn't listening, and as a result, his anxiety had increased. The point here is that salad is neither good nor bad. Salad is either health-supporting or health-weakening, depending on the person and the time of year, and your internal voice knows whether it is health-supporting or health-weakening for you right now.

---

7. Name and identifying details have been changed to protect the privacy of this individual.

Case Study[8]

Joyce, a 39-year-old woman, was training for a marathon to celebrate her upcoming 40th birthday and was running 5k and 10k races pretty much every weekend. She ended up severely injured even though she had trained carefully and was in relatively good health. She told me there were actually two moments she could distinctly remember, a few weeks before and then again a few hours before her injury, when her internal voice told her to slow down, but she ignored it both times. In this case, running was health-weakening for her because of the time of the year (summer) and because she had been working long hours at work and was having a conflict with a coworker, all of which decreased her body's ability to cope with the physical stress of intensive training. Again, the point here is that running is neither good nor bad. Running is either health-supporting or health-weakening, depending on the person and the time of year.

8. Name and identifying details have been changed to protect the privacy of this individual.

Chapter 13

THE GOLDEN PRINCIPLE

Earlier we discussed the 20 qualities which are organized into 10 pairs of opposites. These qualities are essential to understand the most important principle in Ayurveda, the Golden Principle. This principle tells us how to keep our genetic blueprint, or elemental composition, balanced and how to remedy an active imbalance that is showing up as a single symptom or a few symptoms.

The Golden Principle

LIKE INCREASES LIKE.
OPPOSITES REDUCE.

The Golden Principle says that if you have a symptom with a specific quality and you apply a remedy which has the same quality, you will increase the symptom. However, if you apply a remedy with the opposite quality, you will reduce the symptom. For example, if your symptom has a quality of hot and you use a remedy with a quality of hot, the symptom will be aggravated and will get hotter. Instead, if you use a remedy with a quality of cold, the symptom will be pacified and will get cooler because of the balancing effect of the Golden Principle. This idea can be applied to all 10 pairs of opposite qualities. (See image 13.1.)

For example, if you have anxiety with the quality of mobile, you would choose a remedy with the opposite quality, stable. Choosing exercise that has lots of movement, such as running or vinyasa yoga, would increase the quality of mobile and therefore increase anxiety. This is "like increases like." Instead, choosing exercise that has more stability and is slower, such as walking or restorative yoga, would increase the quality of stable and instead decrease anxiety. This is "opposites reduce."

Another example is the symptom of a rash with the quality of hot. As discussed above, adding a remedy with the quality of hot, such as foods that are spicy, would increase the quality of hot and increase the rash. This is "like increases like." Instead, foods that have the quality of cold—those with a high water content, such as melon, cucumbers, and celery—decrease rash. This is "opposites reduce."

The Golden Principle lies at the heart of the idea of "counterbalancing" and The Counterbalance Solution™, which we will go into greater detail in part 4. The beauty of this principle is that because it's simple, it makes Ayurveda a powerful health catalyst that everyone can use to reawaken the healer within, transform symptoms, and achieve optimal wellness.

LIKE INCREASES LIKE.

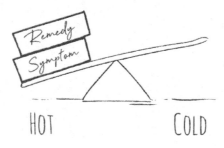

HOT   COLD

OPPOSITES REDUCE.

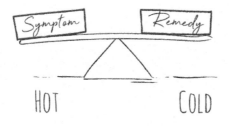

HOT   COLD

Image 13.1 Applying the Golden Principle

PART 3

Ayurveda for Everyone

"Nothing is right for everyone and
everything is right for someone."

—*Ayurvedic Proverb*

Chapter 14

WRITE YOUR OWN PRESCRIPTION

The ability to listen to what we need is something we all are born with. Think about children. They listen to themselves. They cry and seek comfort when they're hurt. They eat when they're hungry. They sleep when they're tired. However, as children grow older, they begin to lose this ability to listen, and eventually, as adults, they can't even hear what their inner voice is saying. They are taught to believe that someone or something outside of them will give them all the answers they are looking for. Ayurveda is about relearning how to listen to what we need.

Listening to what we need is a daily practice, not just something we should do when we have obvious symptoms. It's a daily practice of course correction in which we consider how we are feeling, reflect on why we're feeling what we're feeling, and then make adjustments to move toward balance.

When we transform our relationship to our symptoms, however subtle or obvious they may be, by hearing what they are saying and considering why they are showing up, we take back our health—and maintain it.

Three primary remedies are used to support health in Ayurveda—routines (*vihara*), diet (*ahara*), and tools of yoga (*yoga*), which I will discuss in greater detail in the following three chapters. However, it's not enough to learn about these remedies intellectually and then try to apply them according to a formula to relieve symptoms. Instead, listening to the healer within to choose remedies facilitates exponential and powerful healing. (See image 14.1.)

Although we can seek out information and guides that can help us decrease our suffering, ultimately, each of us can write our own prescription for self-healing.

Remedies for Healing

Routines
SEASONAL
DAILY

Diet
FOOD 'FARMACY'
SPICE 'MEDICINE CABINET'

Tools of Yoga
BREATH WORK
POSTURE
MEDITATION

Image 14.1 Remedies for Healing

Chapter 15

ROUTINES FOR HEALTH

Routines are crucial for health.

The essence of Ayurveda is that we are not separate from nature. Therefore, when we live in harmony with nature, we have optimal and vibrant health.

One way that we can live in harmony with nature is by living in harmony with the rhythms of nature by using routines. The two main rhythms of nature are daily and seasonal, making daily routines (dinacharya) and seasonal routines (ritucharya) crucial for health.

In Ayurveda, daily and seasonal routines are the foundation to maintaining health. In fact, routines are the most powerful remedy in Ayurveda because they help maintain *and regain* health. Among the first recommendations I give anyone who comes to see me, regardless of their symptoms or challenges, is to make adjustments to their daily routine. Something as simple as committing to a regular bedtime and wake time, adjusting the timing of meals, or moving specific work tasks from morning to afternoon can create profound shifts. The impact on health that I have seen by living in sync with the daily and seasonal rhythms of nature still amazes me to this day. (See image 15.1.)

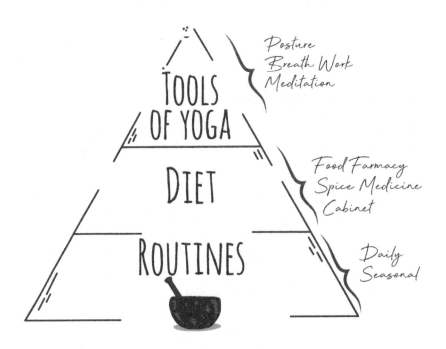

Image 15.1 Foundation of Health

My children will tell you that I always say, "Timing is everything." And it is quite literally so in Ayurveda. Depending on what the predominant qualities are of a certain time of day or season of the year, there are specific activities that are health-supporting for everyone, which is what I will focus on here. The accumulation of qualities from one stage to the next stage of each rhythm of nature affects us by influencing our elemental composition, putting us out of balance and showing up as symptoms if we don't course-correct.

This means we must be aware of the rhythms of nature and how they're affecting our health—specifically, how we're feeling from hour to hour, from day to day, from week to week, and from month to month.

Therefore, as we live with and through the rhythms of nature, we must adjust or transition our routines to maintain optimal health.

Daily routines.

The Ayurvedic clock is helpful to understand the daily rhythm of nature because it shows the 24-hour daily cycle in terms of the elements and their qualities. In the above image, the top half is daytime and the bottom half is nighttime. Each half is divided into pie wedges, or 4-hour blocks, each with an element that predominates during that block. As you can see, there is an air, fire, and earth time block during each half of the day, in which the qualities of the predominant element will accumulate. Therefore, the activities that are best during that time are those that use the associated qualities to support health, forming the basic framework of the daily routine. Please note that the times listed are suggested times. If you vary by 30 to 90 minutes, it's absolutely fine. Let's go through each 4-hour block, starting at the lower left of the image where the star is. (See image 15.2.)

Ayurvedic Clock

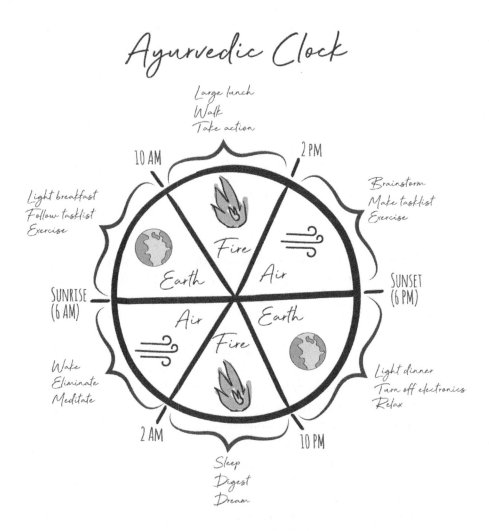

Image 15.2 Ayurvedic Clock

2 a.m. to 6 a.m.

From 2 a.m. to 6 a.m., the element of air, which is all about movement, predominates. Qualities of cold, light, dry, and mobile will accumulate near the end of the block. The activities that support health during this time block are those that tap into the energy of movement, specifically the quality of mobile.

1. *Wake up with the sun and make your bed.* Waking up with the sun and accomplishing a task first thing in the morning helps to build momentum as you move into your day. Because your brain releases dopamine when you achieve goals, something as simple as making your bed provides a dopamine hit right away. Since dopamine improves attention, memory, and motivation, achieving this one small goal can result in a positive feedback loop that makes you more motivated to work harder going forward.

2. *Remove toxins from your sense organs and empty your bowels.* During sleep, your body is going through an internal cleansing cycle in which waste and toxins are being processed for elimination. To help to finish the job, it's important to flush out the toxins that accumulate overnight in the sense organs and the GI tract. When you wake up, rinse your eyes and mouth with warm water, scrape your tongue using a tongue scraper, and flush your nose using a nasal saline flush bulb or neti pot. Also empty your bowels as early as possible in the morning. Drinking warm water with lemon upon waking stimulates peristalsis in the GI tract, which gets things moving.

3. *Prime your system with 3–10 minutes of exercise.* "Priming" is a way to activate the body and the brain to be in an optimal state before starting the day. Peak performers know that what they do first thing in the morning sets the tone for the day ahead. Any kind of movement of the spine is a way to prime your body because it creates the movement of life force energy (*prana*) through the system, decreases stress hormones, and increases the flow of glucose and oxygen to the brain to fire up energy production. An easy way to do this is with a few rounds of sun salutations (*surya namaskar*), a posture sequence in which the spine is moved in every direction.

6 a.m. to 10 a.m.

From 6 a.m. to 10 a.m., the element of earth, which is all about stability, predominates. Qualities of sticky, heavy, cold, and stable will accumulate near the end of the block. During this time block, activities that counterbalance (oppose) the static and heavy earth qualities (that can prevent active participation in life) will support health.

1. *Follow a task list.* By starting a prewritten task list and focusing on three important things, you're creating more dopamine hits to your brain to continue creating a positive feedback loop so you can be more productive all day long. An added benefit is that you don't have to think hard about what to do.
2. *Eat a breakfast that is light and easy to digest.* Because the earth qualities of sticky, heavy, cold, and stable are stronger than the qualities of the digestive fire at the start of the day, it's best to eat a light, warm, and easy-to-digest breakfast. Something cooked, like oatmeal or stewed apples and pears, is ideal.
3. *Do exercise that increases your heart rate.* If you prefer to exercise earlier in the day, this is the ideal time to do so because the mobile quality of exercise will counterbalance the static quality of this first earth time of the day.

10 a.m. to 2 p.m.

From 10 a.m. to 2 p.m., the element of fire, which is all about transformation, predominates. Qualities of hot, sharp, oily, and mobile will accumulate near the end of the block. During this time block, your digestive fire is very high, so activities that support health are all related to the midday meal of lunch. Remember, you can break these down and just do one thing at a time. Over time, you'll create a lunch routine that has all of these elements to support your health.

1. *Make lunch your largest meal.* This is the time when your digestive fire is strongest, making it the best time to eat the largest and heaviest meal of the day. Adding some healthy fats to lunch can speed up your metabolism, make your brain work better, and balance your hormones. Some healthy fats are grass-fed, organic, and sustainably raised lamb, beef, and chicken;

pasture-raised eggs; grass-fed butter or ghee; unsweetened nut and seed milks/butters; nuts like almonds, walnuts, and pecans; avocados; and extra-virgin olive oil.

2. ***When you eat—eat. No distractions.*** This means you're focused on eating . . . not on working, not on your phone, and not on reading a book. Take at least a 30-minute lunch break and eat in a relaxed manner while sitting at a table . . . not at your desk in front of the computer, not in your car, and not while you're walking. Focusing on eating sends a signal to your body to prepare itself for the food, increasing your satisfaction, which, in turn, allows you to eat only what you need.

3. ***Take a "thank you" walk after lunch.*** Research shows that you can't be stressed and thankful at the same time. When you combine gratitude and physical exercise, you tap into a very powerful source of energy, creativity, and positivity. Your brain becomes flooded with natural antidepressant neurochemicals and your mind and body are filled with positive emotions. When you take this walk right after lunch, you'll also avoid the dreaded afternoon slump and instead feel alert, creative, and energized. Ten minutes a day is all it takes. We all have 10 minutes. Take a thank you walk. You'll be so grateful you did.

2 p.m. to 6 p.m.

From 2 p.m. to 6 p.m., once again the element of air predominates. Qualities of cold, light, dry, and mobile will accumulate near the end of the block. The activities that support health during this time block are those that include movement—of both the mind and the body.

1. ***Brainstorm and strategize.*** The air element, which is all about movement, supports creativity and expansive thinking. Therefore, this is a great time to engage in creative pursuits, brainstorming, and problem solving.

2. ***Make a list and plan tomorrow.*** This is related to the activity above because you're tapping into the quality of mobile or increased nervous system activity, which allows creativity and expansive thinking to peak, which then makes creating a task list for the following day a lot easier.

3. *Do exercise that increases your heart rate.* If you prefer to exercise later in the day, this is the ideal time to do so because the mobile quality of exercise will tap into the mobile quality of this time of the day. Be sure not to exercise too late, as you risk disrupting the relaxation that comes with the second earth time of the day, which begins at 6 p.m.

6 p.m. to 10 p.m.

From 6 p.m. to 10 p.m., once again the element of earth predominates. Qualities of sticky, heavy, cold, and stable will accumulate near the end of the block. The most important activities during this time block are those that tap into the static and heavy earth qualities, helping you wind down from the day to prepare your body, mind, and spirit for sleep.

1. *Observe a "tech sabbath."* Unplug and turn off anything that glows at a set time, like 8 p.m. Make it a habit to avoid computers, smartphones, tablets, and television for at least 1 to 2 hours before bed. Studies show that the bright, artificial, high-spectrum blue light that's emitted from electronics can disrupt brain activity and alter sleep hormones like melatonin. By spending your evenings winding down from the day without technology and electronics, you're tapping into the quality of stable. You'll find that, over time, this will help decrease your stress and improve your sleep. A helpful tip is to actually set an alarm on your devices to remind you to turn them off.

2. *Follow an evening routine.* In the same way that the right morning routine can set you up for a productive day, an evening routine that helps you relax can also set you up for success the next day. Connect with family and friends. Do some light pleasurable reading. Listen to music. Reflect on your day with prayer, journaling, or gratitude. Stick to a set time to go to your bedroom to prepare for bedtime.

3. *Eat an early, warm, and light dinner.* The body needs 3 to 4 hours to complete the digestive process, and digestion is slower in the evening. When we eat dinner later than 7 or 8 p.m., we're working with a less efficient and shorter digestive process, which can lead to a feeling of heaviness.

10 p.m. to 2 a.m.

From 10 p.m. to 2 a.m., once again the element of fire, which is all about transformation, predominates. Qualities of hot, sharp, oily, and mobile will accumulate near the end of the block. During this time block, the only activity that supports health is sleep, which taps into the energy of transformation, using the increased digestive fire for the repair processes that occur in the body and mind during the night.

1. *Go to bed by 10 p.m.* I always say, "Your day starts the night before," because sleep is essential to replenish the body, mind, and spirit. The internal body clock, located in the pineal gland, senses changes in daylight via the optic nerves in your eyes. So, as the sun sets, the pineal gland senses diminishing light and secretes the hormone melatonin. As your mind decreases its mental activity through sleep, your body uses the increased digestive fire to begin the internal repair and restoration processes. If you miss the 10 p.m. bedtime, you can feel hungry and get the "midnight munchies" because your brain thinks that this increased digestive fire is asking for food when it's actually getting ready to clean up the toxins in your body. If you're currently going to sleep later than 10 p.m., try to go to sleep 15 minutes earlier every few days until you hit the 10 p.m. goal. When you plan for adequate sleep, you're planning for health and healing.

As you can see, tuning in to the daily rhythm of nature creates a daily routine. By being aware of the predominant qualities that are present in each of the 4-hour time blocks, you can adjust your daily activities to support your health. As I stated before, routines are the most powerful remedy in Ayurveda because they help maintain *and regain* health.

Seasonal routines.

The transitions between seasons are marked by changes in nature—shifts in the weather, changes in the landscape, and migration of animals. During each season, a different element of nature predominates and the qualities of that element accumulate. Therefore, the activities that are best during that season are those that use the predominant qualities to support our health. We primarily counterbalance to cultivate opposite qualities—to prevent overload of the dominant qualities that accumulate during the season—with the routines and activities, or remedy, that we choose. Let's go through each season, starting at the lower right of the diagram where the star is, to learn how to counterbalance to cultivate opposite qualities that will support health. (See image 15.3.)

Late Fall and Winter

During late fall and winter, cold, dry winds are blowing, and thus the predominant element is air, with the qualities of cool, light, dry, and mobile. In nature, we see plants and animals contract, withdraw, hibernate, and pause. They naturally cultivate the opposite qualities of warm, heavy, oily, and stable to counterbalance these qualities of air. In the same way, we must also cultivate these qualities through practices, foods, and movement that are nourishing and grounding to warm up and calm down.

1. **Go inward.** Get in sync with the decreased number of hours of daylight and spend more time indoors. Get more sleep and reflect. These activities cultivate the qualities of warm, heavy, and stable.
2. **Lubricate.** Do a self-massage (*abhyanga*) with warm oil a few times a week to cultivate the qualities of warm, heavy, and oily.
3. **Shift diet.** Include more sweet, sour, salty, heavy, and hot foods and spices. Stews, soups, cooked vegetables, and grains help to cultivate the qualities of warm, heavy, and oily.

Spring

During spring, nature begins to thaw, melt, and soften; thus, the predominant element is earth, with the qualities of sticky, heavy, cool, and stable. To clear out excess mucus, toxins, and stagnation that may have accumulated, we must start heating things up to counterbalance the earth qualities and cultivate qualities of clear, light, warm, and mobile by focusing on practices, foods, and movement that are invigorating, energizing, and dynamic.

1. **Detox.** Reset your system with a 3-day gut rest and eat a mono-diet consisting of foods that are easy to digest such as cooked rice, lentils, and vegetables (*kitchari*). This will cultivate the qualities of light and mobile.

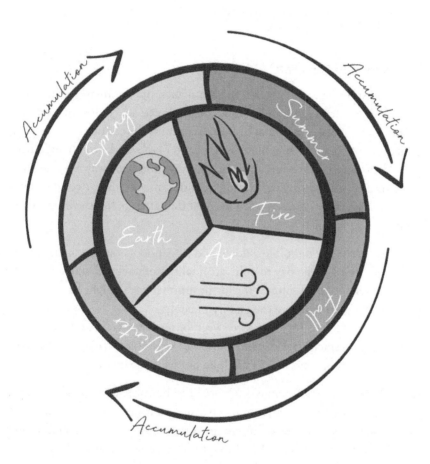

Image 15.3 Seasonal Rhythms

2. *Move energy.* Go for a vigorous walk or practice flow (*vinyasa*)
   yoga to increase the flow of energy (*prana*) through the body,
   which helps clear out toxins that have accumulated and
   cultivates the qualities of light and mobile.
3. *Shift diet.* Include more pungent, spicy, bitter, and astringent
   foods and spices. Leafy greens, broths, and easy-to-digest grains
   such as rice and lentils help to cultivate the qualities of clear,
   warm, and mobile.

Summer and Early Fall

During summer and early fall, the fire element predominates, with qualities of hot, sharp, oily, and mobile. Nature heats up, lights up, and activates, and we see plants and animals intuitively counterbalance these qualities of fire by staying underground and in the shade to cool off during the daytime when the sun burns brightest. In the same way, we must beat the heat of summer by cultivating qualities of cool, dull, dry, and stable through practices, foods, and movement that are fun, lighthearted, sweet, juicy, and playful.

1. *Beat the heat.* Slow down and stay indoors during the hottest
   times of the day to cultivate qualities of cool and stable.
2. *Have fun.* Embrace the joy of summer with a light heart and
   play to cultivate the quality of cool.
3. *Shift diet.* Include more sweet, bitter, astringent, and cool foods
   and spices. Salads with fruits and vegetables that are sweet and
   high in water content help to cultivate the quality of cool.

As you can see, there is a seasonal rhythm of nature. When we tune in and align with this rhythm by choosing routines, foods, and activities that counterbalance the dominant qualities of the season, we support our health to transition smoothly through the different times of the year.

Choosing activities and self-care practices that are in harmony with the daily and seasonal rhythms of nature is the first step when supporting health through routines. By simply making small adjustments to what we are doing and when we are doing things, we can significantly affect our health.

Chapter 16

DIET FOR HEALTH

Food is medicine.

Over the past 10 years, the concept "food is medicine" has gained popularity and acceptance not only among patients but also among medical practitioners. However, it's not a new concept—it has its origin in Ayurveda. In the classical Ayurvedic text, *Charaka Samhita*, believed to have been recorded in 800 BCE, Charaka—one of the principal contributors to Ayurveda—writes,

> **"When diet is wrong, medicine is of no use, and when diet is correct, medicine is of no need."**

The simplicity and brilliance of this statement is profound. A person who eats a wholesome diet in harmony with nature's bounty—food and spices—creates optimal health, and therefore medicine is not needed. However, no medicine will heal a person who does not eat a wholesome diet in harmony with nature. Now I'm not saying that pharmaceutical drugs are not useful. However, I am saying that the effectiveness of those drugs is supported by a diet that is in harmony with nature.

The diet, composed of nature's "food farmacy" and "spice medicine cabinet," is how we harmonize with the bounty of nature. When we assimilate nature's bounty into the body, mind, and spirit, we connect the microcosm to the macrocosm and can have optimal and vibrant health.

The principle of Ayurvedic eating.

Anytime I meet someone or I am teaching students or I am seeing patients, the first question I'm asked is "What should I eat?" Or, more specifically, I'm asked what to eat for a symptom or to lose weight or to increase energy and on and on. And my answer is always the same. What you eat is only one part of the whole picture when using diet as remedy in Ayurveda. What you eat matters. Why, where, when, and how much you eat matters more. This is the principle of Ayurvedic eating, and it's crucial for optimal health.

The Principle of Ayurvedic Eating
What you eat matters.
WHY, WHERE, WHEN, & HOW MUCH
YOU EAT MATTERS MORE.

In Ayurveda, *why* we eat is the most important factor in our relationship to food because it determines how the food will be received by the human system. When we begin to use diet as remedy, or food[9] as medicine, we must become conscious of why we are eating and hold the intention that what we eat will heal us. If subconsciously we eat to buffer or suppress emotions, we are not holding the intention that food can heal us. As a result, what we eat becomes health-weakening instead of health-supporting.

Where we eat also matters greatly according to Ayurveda. It's important to sit down at a table and take at least 30 minutes to eat a meal.

---

9. When I say "food," I am referring to anything we eat or drink—so it includes food, spices, and drinks.

Setting the table—with nice dishes and cloth napkins, a vase of flowers, and some candles—creates a pleasant, quiet, and soothing environment that engages all five of our senses. This then contributes to more enjoyment and nourishment. When we eat standing up, while walking, while sitting in front of the computer, or while in our cars during our commute, we are not paying attention to our meal, which decreases the healing power of food dramatically.

Earlier, we discussed daily routines and learned that *when* and *how much* we eat, which are linked in Ayurveda, also determine whether our food is health-supporting or health-weakening. Eating at the proper times of the day and being mindful of the quantity helps to ensure better digestion, a key to health according to Ayurveda. When we eat on a regular schedule, eat our largest meal at lunch (between 10 a.m. and 2 p.m.) and eat an earlier, lighter, and easier-to-digest breakfast and dinner, we are helping our digestion perform optimally and supporting our health.

And, finally, we come to *what* we eat, the aspect of diet that everyone always focuses on as most important. Clearly, what we eat is only one part of the whole picture when using diet as remedy. The main guideline here is to eat seasonally, because nature knows what to provide during every season to create balance and support health. Just because we can buy strawberries in the grocery store in December doesn't mean we should buy (and then eat) them. Eating food that is not local or seasonal creates imbalance and is health-weakening. If you're not sure what is local or in season, choose fruits and vegetables that are cheaper in the grocery store—a great clue to what is in abundance in nature at that time.

As you can see, when using the diet to support health, it's most important to first consider the *why, where, when,* and *how much* before focusing on the *what*. And even when considering the *what*, the first step is to eat seasonally to tap into nature's intelligence of providing what we need throughout the year to support health.

Chapter 17

TOOLS OF YOGA FOR HEALTH

Yoga reveals patterns of imbalance.

Many of us have come to believe that yoga is all about the postures (*asana*)—the headstands and handstands, the one-leg balancing poses, and the perfect seated, crossed-legged lotus position. However, yoga is so much more than the physical practice of postures. Yoga (in which the postures are just one of many tools) is the sister-science of Ayurveda that has been used to support health for more than 5,000 years. Yoga reveals patterns of imbalance, with the ultimate goal being freedom from these patterns. This freedom, in turn, decreases suffering because our old patterns and habits are what create symptoms, illness, and disease in the first place.

Ultimately, "yoga is not about doing the postures. Instead, yoga is about undoing what's in the way of the postures."[10]

The key to all of this is the breath, because yoga is bringing the mind and the body together through the breath. The breath tells us what's in the way. It tells us what we need to unlearn or change in the patterns or habits of our mind or in the patterns or habits of our body that are

---

10.   Leslie Kaminoff

creating imbalance. It is through the breath that we bring about transformation and healing, or, as we would say in yoga, how we decrease suffering. For example, if you're holding your breath, you can reflect and ask, "Where is this pattern or habit coming from? Is it coming from my body? Is it coming from my mind?" You see, we are multidimensional beings in which everything is connected—and the breath is where the mind and body meet. (See image 17.1.)

By replenishing and moving nature's life force energy (*prana*), through the body, mind, and spirit, the tools of yoga connect the macrocosm to the microcosm and allow us to live in harmony with nature. I will be focusing on the three most important tools of yoga for health and healing—breathwork (*pranayama*), posture (*asana*), and meditation (*dhyana*).[11]

Breathwork.

Breathwork, or *pranayama*,[12] is a technique that breaks unconscious patterns and causes many changes in the physiology of the body and the mind. Therefore, by changing the breath, we can change responses of the body and mind that may be causing imbalance into responses that support health. For example, when someone's breath is tense, shallow, or erratic, slowing down the breath to more easeful, long, and smooth inhales and exhales will turn down the stress response and activate the relaxation response instead. (See image 17.2.)

There are four parts of the breath: the inhale, the pause after the inhale, the exhale, and the pause after the exhale. The inhale is activating. The exhale is calming.

The most basic thing to remember is that when you lengthen either part of the breath, the effect of that part of the breath will show up in the body and mind.

---

11. I'll also talk about some other tools of yoga in combination with the first three tools. Those include visualization (*bhavana*) and sound or affirmation (*mantra*).
12. *Prana* means vital life force and *yama* means to extend. So *pranayama* means to extend the vital life force.

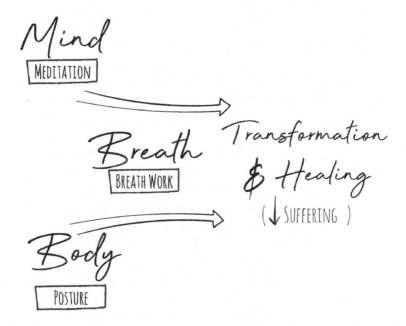

Image 17.1 Breath Is the Key

Inhale

INHALE - (PAUSE)

Activating

- STABILIZES MOOD (DEPRESSION)
- INCREASES ENERGY
- INCREASES FOCUS + ATTENTION
- HEATING (SUN)

Exhale

EXHALE - (PAUSE)

Calming

- REDUCES ANXIETY + OVERWHELM
- CALMS ANGER + IRRITABILITY
- EASES PAIN
- PROMOTES SLEEP
- COOLING (MOON)

Image 17.2 The Breath

Inhale

Exhale

INHALE	- (PAUSE)	EXHALE	- (PAUSE)
2	0	3	0
(4)	0	3	0
2	0	(4)	0

Image 17.3 Lengthening the Breath

If you lengthen the inhale, you tap into the activating effect of the breath. If you lengthen the exhale, you tap into the calming effect of the breath. Lengthening the breath simply means extending the duration or count of the inhale part or the exhale part of the breath.

For example, if your natural inhale is a count of two, extending the count to three is "lengthening the inhale" and you tap into the activating effect of the breath on the body and mind. The activating effects include stabilization of mood and depression, an increase of energy, and improved concentration. Anytime you want to get yourself moving and energized or want to lift your mood, extend the inhale part of the breath. This technique is very useful in the morning to get going and in the afternoon to increase focus. (See image 17.3.)

Now let's move to the exhale. If your natural exhale is a count of three, extending the count to four is "lengthening the exhale" and you tap into the calming effect of the breath on the body and mind. The calming effects include reduction of anxiety and overwhelm, decrease of anger, and relief of pain. Any time you are feeling irritable or anxious, extend the exhale part of the breath. This technique is very useful throughout the day to control stress and at night to promote sleep.

This simple framework of breathwork is one that you can use anytime and anywhere. Once you begin using this basic practice, you can begin to add on more advanced techniques. But don't be fooled into thinking that more advanced equals more powerful.

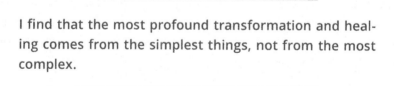

I find that the most profound transformation and healing comes from the simplest things, not from the most complex.

Posture.

As I said earlier, yoga is not just about the posture, or *asana*. Posture is one of many tools of yoga, but it has become the focus of yoga in the West. In addition, the purpose of posture is not to look like the cover model on the latest yoga magazine or to have perfect alignment. The purpose is to maintain a steady and comfortable state when in the posture. This requires not only a strong and flexible body but also a long, easeful, smooth breath and a focused, attentive mind. If you don't have a steady and comfortable posture, start to reflect and become curious. Observe your breath and ask yourself whether your discomfort is coming from your body or from your mind. Remember, the breath is where the body and the mind meet, so it provides valuable information about the patterns and habits that cause imbalance. (See image 17.4.)

When I started this discussion of yoga, I said that the tools of yoga connect the microcosm to the macrocosm because they harness, replenish, and move the life-force energy of nature through our body, mind, and spirit. Although each posture has other specific effects, all postures share the effect of increased flow of life-force energy, which supports health in general.

This is why the most important thing when doing any posture is to link the breath and move dynamically with the inhale and exhale.

I find that many people believe that they cannot "do yoga" because they aren't strong enough or flexible enough to do the postures. And here's what I always tell them. Even if your movement is small or slight, if you can link your breath and move dynamically with your inhale and exhale, you can do any posture. Remember, profound transformation and healing comes from small and simple things.

If you can move your body and if you can breathe, you can do postures.

How to do Postures

LINK TO THE BREATH.

Move dynamically with inhale and exhale.

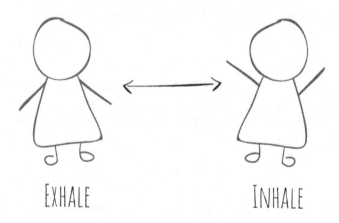

EXHALE   INHALE

Image 17.4 How to Do Postures

Meditation.

The last tool of yoga we will discuss is meditation, or *dhyana,* which means "to merge with what is being focused on." That is to say, to merge the mind with a point of attention. Meditation cultivates a state of aware-ness that can be directed inward to support health. Some of the effects of meditation, which have been widely studied and documented, are that it reduces anxiety and increases serotonin production to increase posi-tive mood, slows the respiratory rate, lowers blood pressure, eases muscle tension, relieves headaches, enhances the immune system, and, most importantly, decreases the perception of stress, thereby creating a greater sense of relaxation.

Everywhere I teach, I'm always asked about meditation. Most people think they can't meditate because they "can't empty their mind" or can't sit in a lotus position on a cushion on the floor. And the truth is, if you're alive, you can't empty your mind, because you can't stop thinking. It's also not necessary to sit on the floor to meditate. (See image 17.5.)

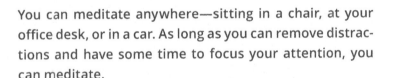

You can meditate anywhere—sitting in a chair, at your office desk, or in a car. As long as you can remove distrac-tions and have some time to focus your attention, you can meditate.

Meditation is not complicated. It's actually very simple. You just focus on something—an object, a visualization,[13] or an affirmation[14] that you repeat silently in your mind. Any time your attention wanders, you gently direct your attention back to what you're focusing on. It's really that simple.

Using the tools of yoga to support health starts with breathwork because the breath is where the body and the mind meet. By observing the breath, you gain information about the patterns or habits that are causing imbalance. Next, link the breath to postures, moving dynamically with the inhale and exhale. If you're having difficulty breathing or doing a posture,

---

13. Visualization, or *bhavana,* is also a commonly used tool of yoga.
14. Affirmation, a form of sound or *mantra,* is also a commonly used tool of yoga.

How to Meditate

FOCUS ON SOMETHING.

Put attention on an object,
visualization or affirmation.

Image 17.5 How to Meditate

look at the mind and whether it's focused on negative thoughts. Most of us are engaged in patterns of negative thoughts, which decrease our focus, making it difficult to breathe and making it difficult to do postures. Create some time and a space that is free of distractions to allow yourself to bring your attention to a point of focus. A daily practice of just 10 to 15 minutes using these three tools of yoga can transform your health.

Chapter 18

HOW TO MAINTAIN HEALTH

As I discussed earlier, routines are the foundation to maintaining health. I always suggest that before you make any changes, you first consider your current daily routine. Think about your typical day and write down what you do and how you feel throughout the day. Now, compare your notes to the activities that support health during each 4-hour time block on the Ayurvedic clock. Are there any changes you can make? Can you adjust when you go to bed or when you wake up? Can you adjust your mealtimes? Can you adjust when you do various tasks at work (such as following a task list, having meetings, or working on new projects)? Can you adjust when you exercise or when you begin to unwind and relax at the end of the day? Jot down any changes you would be willing to make. It's important to emphasize the word "willing"—because you must have the desire to make the change.

Next, pick just one change you are willing to make and link it to something you are already doing on a daily basis. This is a powerful way to create and stick to new habits that will support your health.

For example, if you want to meditate for 10 minutes every morning, link it to making your morning cup of coffee. While your coffee is brewing, sit in a chair in the kitchen, set a timer for 10 minutes, and close your eyes. You want to set yourself up for small wins, and the surest way to do this is to build upon whatever you're already doing and winning at every day.

There is a saying that "knowledge is power, but knowledge without action is useless." And as you might have guessed by now, I'm all about action. Just *knowing* what to do will not give you health; you have to put those methods into practice to see the benefits. I believe deeply in the power of small changes that slowly lead to significant results that not only help you regain health but also help you maintain health. When you make small changes based on the wisdom of Ayurveda, you will experience powerful and significant transformation.

PART 4

You Can Heal Yourself

"It's supposed to be a secret, but I'll tell you anyway. We doctors do nothing. We only help and encourage the doctor within."

—*Albert Schweitzer, MD*

Chapter 19

THE COUNTERBALANCE
SOLUTION™

The beauty and brilliance of Ayurveda is that it is simple and intuitive. However, over the past few years as Ayurveda has attracted more interest in the West, I have been hearing from more and more patients and students that Ayurveda is too complicated to understand or too impractical to put into practice. These concerns are the reason that I wanted to figure out a simpler way to not only explain the principles of Ayurveda but, more importantly, to create a framework to use these ancient principles in modern life.

The result is The Counterbalance Solution™, my practical and highly actionable three-step system to apply the wisdom of Ayurveda for self-healing. The first step is to identify your symptom—physical, mental, or emotional—and its qualities. Next, apply the Golden Principle to determine which qualities you need to cultivate to reduce your symptom and support your health. Last, choose the appropriate remedy or remedies that will cultivate the qualities needed.

THE COUNTERBALANCE™ SOLUTION

1 - IDENTIFY YOUR SYMPTOM (PHYSICAL, MENTAL, OR EMOTIONAL) AND ITS QUALITIES

2 - APPLY THE 'GOLDEN PRINCIPLE.'

   Like increases like.

   Opposites reduce.

3 - CHOOSE REMEDIES TO CULTIVATE THE <u>OPPOSITE</u> QUALITIES.

In part 2, I reviewed the qualities that describe everything in nature.

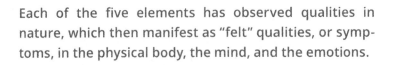

Each of the five elements has observed qualities in nature, which then manifest as "felt" qualities, or symptoms, in the physical body, the mind, and the emotions.

Instead of using measurements, in Ayurveda we describe symptoms according to how we experience them—how they feel and behave. Let's go through each step with some examples to illustrate. (See image 19.1.)

Step 1—Identify your symptom (physical, mental, or emotional) and its qualities.

For simplicity, identify just *one* symptom and its qualities. For example, you might choose insomnia, which has the qualities of cold, light, dry, and mobile like the element of air. If you choose heartburn, it has the qualities of hot, sharp, oily, and mobile like the element of fire. Or perhaps you might choose congestion, which shares the qualities of sticky, heavy, cold, and stable with the element of earth.

Step 2—Apply the Golden Principle.

Using the Golden Principle, "like increases like and opposites reduce," determine which qualities you need to cultivate to counterbalance and reduce the symptom.

Continuing with the examples above in step 1, for insomnia, the opposite qualities are hot, heavy, oily, and stable. For heartburn, the opposite qualities are cold, dull, dry, and stable. And for congestion, the opposite qualities are clear, light, hot, and mobile.

Step 3—Choose remedies to cultivate the opposite qualities.

Now you can choose remedies that will cultivate these opposite qualities that you've identified. The first remedy is routine, which includes daily and seasonal activities. The second remedy is diet, which includes the "food farmacy" and "spice medicine cabinet." And the third remedy includes tools of yoga—posture, breathwork, and meditation.

For simplicity, let's focus on the second remedy of diet in the examples above. A remedy for insomnia that would cultivate the opposite qualities of hot, heavy, oily, and stable would be to eat warm, cooked foods whenever possible. A powerful remedy to reduce heartburn and cultivate the opposite qualities of cold, dull, dry, and stable would be to decrease caffeine, sugar, red meat, and alcohol in the diet. And finally, a remedy to reduce congestion by cultivating the opposite qualities of clear, light, hot, and mobile would be to increase consumption of cooked leafy green vegetables with rice and broth.

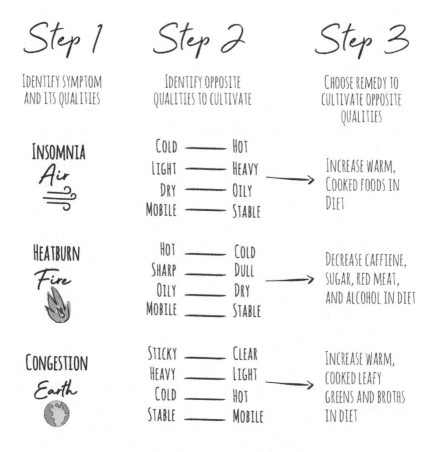

Image 19.1 The Counterbalance Solution™

Case Study

Anxiety is a symptom that I see very commonly in patients and that my students constantly ask me about. Let's go through this example step by step to clarify further. (See image 19.2.)

Step 1—Identify your symptom and its qualities.

Anxiety is considered a mental and emotional symptom. It has the qualities of air, which are cold, light, dry, and mobile.

Step 2—Apply the Golden Principle.

Using the Golden Principle, "like increases like and opposites reduce," to counterbalance and reduce anxiety, we need to cultivate the opposite qualities of hot, heavy, oily, and stable. These are also the qualities of earth, and cultivating them creates a "grounding" effect for the anxiety that is "up in the air."

Step 3—Choose remedies to cultivate the opposite qualities.

Now we can choose remedies that cultivate these opposite qualities of hot, heavy, oily, and stable. The first remedy is routine, both seasonal and daily activities. The second remedy is diet, which includes the "food farmacy" and "spice medicine cabinet." And the third remedy includes tools of yoga—posture, breathwork, and meditation.

To cultivate a "grounding" quality of stable, it's important to have a daily routine. Many people who have anxiety say that they have very irregular schedules that have a lot of "movement." Creating regularity—regular mealtimes and regular waking and sleeping times—creates a feeling of stability, which helps to reduce anxiety. Another routine that cultivates the qualities of hot, heavy, and oily is self-massage with warm oil (*abhyanga*).

Let's move on to the second remedy, which is diet. Many people who have a lot of anxiety tend to like foods with cold and dry qualities, such as raw foods/salads. To cultivate the opposite qualities of hot, heavy, oily, and stable, increasing warm, cooked foods such as stews, made with root vegetables sautéed in oil and warming spices of ginger and pepper, helps decrease anxiety. In addition, sipping warm water throughout the day also cultivates the quality of hot.

The third remedy is the tools of yoga. To cultivate the qualities of heavy and stable, restorative, seated, and supine poses that are "grounding" help reduce anxiety significantly. Other tools of yoga that cultivate opposite qualities of hot, heavy, and stable are exhale-focused breathing, gratitude meditation, or meditation upon a visualization of mountains or tree roots to pull that movement of anxiety down to ground it.

By using The Counterbalance Solution™, you can write your own prescription for self-healing and optimal health. I have already discussed the three areas of remedies as they apply to maintaining health. Now, let's dive a little deeper and discuss them as they apply to symptoms.

CASE STUDY - ANXIETY

1 - IDENTIFY YOUR SYMPTOM (PHYSICAL, MENTAL, OR EMOTIONAL) AND ITS QUALITIES.

Anxiety ⟶ Air ⟶ Cold, light, dry, mobile

2- APPLY THE 'GOLDEN PRINCIPLE' TO IDENTIFY THE OPPOSITE QUALITIES TO CULTIVATE.

⟶ Hot, heavy, oily, stable

3- CHOOSE REMEDIES TO CULTIVATE THE OPPOSITE QUALITIES.

ROUTINES : Regular wake/sleep, regular meal times, abhyangha massage

DIET : Warm cooked foods, warm water, ginger/cinnamon

TOOLS OF YOGA : Restorative yoga, grounding poses on floor (seated + supine), exhale-focused breathing, gratitude meditation (mountains + trees)

Image 19.2 Case Study—Anxiety

Chapter 20

ROUTINES AS REMEDY

In Ayurveda, routines that align with the rhythms of nature form the foundation of health.

So, it's important to pause to consider whether the symptom you're experiencing is being influenced by nature's rhythms or whether it is being caused by a misalignment between your routines and nature's rhythms.

In either case, an adjustment to your daily or seasonal routines forms the foundation of the remedies you need to counterbalance your symptom.

Case Study

For example, you develop a rash in the middle of July, 2 weeks before an important client presentation you've been preparing for the past 3 months, during which you've regularly been working 60-hour weeks. Let's go through the three steps of The Counterbalance Solution™ to illustrate how we can use routines as remedy in this case. (See image 20.1.)

Step 1—Identify your symptom and its qualities.

Rash is a physical symptom with qualities of hot, sharp, and mobile. For simplicity, we will focus on just one quality of rash—the quality of hot. Summer is the seasonal rhythm with qualities of hot and sharp. Working 60 hours every week for 3 months is a daily activity with qualities of hot, sharp, and mobile.

Step 2—Apply the Golden Principle.

If we apply the Golden Principle of "like increases like and opposites reduce," we see that summer and 60-hour work weeks both have the quality of hot and rash is also a symptom with the quality of hot. In the case of rash and summer, nature's seasonal rhythm is influencing the appearance of the symptom. In the case of rash and 60-hour work weeks, misalignment between the daily routine and nature's daily rhythm of day and night is causing the symptom. To reduce the quality of hot, you must cultivate the quality of cold.

Step 3—Choose remedies to cultivate the opposite qualities.

Given that you cannot change the season, and assuming you cannot change your job immediately, to cultivate the opposite quality of cold using remedy as routine, you could

1. Limit time outdoors—slow down and stay indoors during the hottest times of the day
2. Choose fun—add play and creativity to your day
3. Take a moonbath—walk in the light of the moon, which has cooling energy

The key here is to remember that every routine has qualities, and by choosing routines that counterbalance your symptom, you can use routines as remedy. The routines that follow are ones I commonly prescribe, which have been organized by the quality/qualities they cultivate.

CASE STUDY - RASH

1 - IDENTIFY YOUR SYMPTOM (PHYSICAL, MENTAL, OR EMOTIONAL) AND ITS QUALITIES.

Rash ⟶ Fire ⟶ (Hot) sharp, oily, mobile

2- APPLY THE 'GOLDEN PRINCIPLE' TO IDENTIFY THE <u>OPPOSITE</u> QUALITIES TO CULTIVATE.

⟶ Cold

3- CHOOSE REMEDIES TO CULTIVATE THE <u>OPPOSITE</u> QUALITIES.

ROUTINES : Limit time outdoors, choose fun, take a moonbath

Image 20.1 Case Study—Rash

The qualities of routines.

Heavy

- Self-massage (*abhyanga*)—apply warm oil from head to toe with light pressure
- "Earth" your feet—walk barefoot in the grass
- Soothe your soles—massage your feet and apply warm oil to your soles before bed
- Sleep earlier—move your bedtime up by 30 minutes

Light

- Wake up earlier—set your alarm clock 30 minutes earlier
- Walk and talk—take a walk in nature with a friend and "hug trees"
- Have fun—get creative, add play, and ditch the competition
- Tidy up—clear the clutter in your home

Hot

- Cultivate warmth—stay indoors as much as possible
- Dress warmly—always cover your head and neck when outdoors
- Get heat—spend 10 minutes in an infrared sauna (dry heat)
- Sunbathe—sit in the sun for 10 to 15 minutes

Cold

- Get out early—spend time outdoors in the early morning or late evening
- Refresh with rose—spray your skin with rosewater throughout the day
- Dress lightly—wear clothing in light colors and fabrics (linen, cotton)
- Moonbathe—sit/walk in the light of the moon for 10 to 15 minutes

Stable

- Get regular—follow a consistent schedule, start with wake/bedtimes or mealtimes
- "Earth" your feet—walk barefoot in the grass
- Have a siesta—nap in the afternoon for 10 to 15 minutes
- Soothe your soles—massage your feet and apply warm oil to your soles before bed

Mobile

- Get moving—take a brisk walk outdoors in the early morning or afternoon
- Rub your tummy—massage your abdomen to encourage digestion
- Drink all day—take sips of warm/room temperature water every 10 to 15 minutes to keep things moving
- Let it out—don't suppress natural urges (burps, hiccups, gas, etc. are natural)

Chapter 21

DIET AS REMEDY

Before we get into the specifics of *what* to eat or which foods to use as remedy, it's important to understand the distinction between Western nutrition and Ayurvedic nutrition. In Western nutrition, food is measured by its biochemical components of calories, grams of carbohydrates, fats, and proteins, or milligrams of vitamins and minerals. This gives us quantitative information about the basic chemistry of the food we consume.

Ayurvedic nutrition, however, is focused on the *qualities* of food, which give us experiential information and create a sense of nourishment.

Instead of using measurements, we describe food according to how we experience it—how it tastes, feels, and acts. That's how we connect with food. For example, you'll say, "I want something sweet" more often than "I want something with a few grams of sugar." Or you'll say, "Wow, this feels heavy in my stomach," not "My stomach is filled with too many grams of protein and carbohydrates." (See image 21.1.)

The shift here is thinking about nourishment instead of consumption, which may be a huge perspective change for many of you. Consumption considers how the chemistry of food affects us. Nourishment considers how the qualities of food heal us.

Feel

- Before you eat it
- After a few bites
- 20 Qualities

Heavy	——	Light
Dull	——	Sharp
Hot	——	Cold
Oily	——	Dry
Smooth	——	Rough
Solid	——	Liquid
Hard	——	Soft
Stable	——	Mobile
Gross	——	Subtle
Sticky	——	Clear

Taste

- First Impression on tongue
- 6 tastes

Act

- Reaction created after eating
- Energy released
- Heating or Cooling

Image 21.1 Qualities of Food

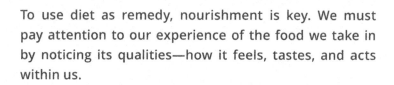

To use diet as remedy, nourishment is key. We must pay attention to our experience of the food we take in by noticing its qualities—how it feels, tastes, and acts within us.

Then we can begin to get more specific and choose foods as remedy based on the qualities we want to cultivate to counterbalance a specific symptom.

One quick tip—when choosing foods as remedy, first focus just on the way food feels. When you have a good sense of the way food feels, then move on to the way food tastes, and finally to the way food acts. It's easy to get confused trying to consider all three ways we experience food together when using diet as remedy.

The qualities of food.

The way food feels

Let's start with the way food feels. This is how you would describe it before you eat it and is something you sense even before you put it in your mouth. In Ayurveda, we describe the way food feels using the 20 qualities I've already talked about.

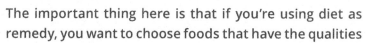

The important thing here is that if you're using diet as remedy, you want to choose foods that have the qualities you're trying to cultivate.

For example, to cultivate the quality of heavy, you might choose meat or dairy (milk, cheese), whereas to cultivate the quality of light, you might choose popcorn or leafy greens. To cultivate the quality of hot, you might choose ginger, chilies, garlic, or alcohol, but to cultivate the quality of cold, you might choose mint or cucumbers. Below is a list of common foods used as remedy, organized by the qualities they cultivate. (See image 21.2.)

Heavy	MEAT, FRIED FOODS, DAIRY, CHEESE, SWEETS, WHEAT	Light	POPCORN, LEAFY GREENS
Dull	FATS, MEAT	Sharp	GARLIC, GINGER, PEPPERS, RADISH, ONION
Cold	ICE CREAM, CHILLED MILK, CHILLED DRINKS	Hot	GINGER, CHILLIES, GARLIC, ALCOHOL
Oily	BUTTER, GHEE, OILS, AVOCADO	Dry	BARLEY, TOASTED BREAD, POPCORN, NUTRITION BARS
Smooth	RICE FLOUR, ALL CREAMY FOODS	Rough	RAW FOODS, DRIED FRUITS, POPCORN, CHIPS
Solid	ROOT VEGETABLES, NUTS, GRAINS, MEAT	Liquid	ALL FLUIDS - WATER, MILK, JUICE, BROTH
Soft	BANANA, AVOCADO, FIG, BUTTER, GHEE	Hard	NUTS, CRACKERS, CHIPS
Stable	MEAT WITH BONES, WHEAT, GHEE	Mobile	LAXATIVE FOODS, LEAFY VEGETABLES
Sticky	HONEY, MOLASSES, SYRUP	Clear	WATERY FOODS, BROTH
Gross	MEAT, GRAINS	Subtle	ALCOHOL

Image 21.2 The Way Food Feels

The way food tastes

The second property of food is taste. Taste is the first impression you get on your tongue when you put food into your mouth. In Ayurveda, there are six tastes: sweet, sour, salty, bitter, pungent, and astringent.

Each taste aligns with specific elements and therefore cultivates those elements' qualities.

Sweet taste aligns with earth (and water) and primarily cultivates the qualities of sticky, heavy, cold, and stable. It creates feelings of pleasure and comfort. One note—sweet doesn't mean sugar. Think more of the natural sweetness inherent in grains, dairy, fruits, and vegetables.

Sour taste aligns with fire (and earth) and primarily cultivates the qualities of hot, sharp, oily, and mobile. It cleanses and energizes the body's tissues and also stimulates the digestive fire, which makes it a great taste in a condiment or an appetizer. You'll recognize sour taste because your mouth will fill with saliva and heat. Some sour foods are tomatoes, lemons, tart berries, most unripe fruits, yogurt, pickles, and fermented foods.

Salty taste aligns with fire (and water) and primarily cultivates the qualities of hot, sharp, oily, and mobile. It improves digestion/absorption by lubricating and clearing obstructions in the digestive channels. Foods with salty taste are all types of salt, as well as sea vegetables such as nori, dulse, kombu, and tamari.

Bitter taste aligns with air (and space) and primarily cultivates the qualities of cold, light, dry, and mobile. It is the taste that overrides the others and has a cleansing effect. It's generally not a favorite of most people, but in small amounts you might actually crave it. Bitter taste is present in coffee, dark leafy greens, and spices such as fenugreek and turmeric.

Pungent taste aligns with fire (and air) and primarily cultivates the qualities of hot, sharp, oily, and mobile. It excites all the senses and gets things moving along, thereby stimulating digestion. Pungent foods are mostly spices including garlic, ginger, mustard seeds, and all kinds of pepper, as well as vegetables such as onions, radishes, and turnips.

Astringent taste aligns with air (and earth) and primarily cultivates the qualities of cold, light, dry, and mobile. It contracts the tissues and creates a cleansing effect. Astringent foods make you pucker, sucking the water out of your mouth, and include cruciferous vegetables (broccoli, cauliflower, cabbage), pomegranate, cranberries, apples, pears, green tea, red wine, and honey. (See image 21.3.)

Sweet	GRAINS, DAIRY, FRUITS, VEGETABLES
Sour	TOMATOES, LEMONS, TART BERRIES, MOST UNRIPE FRUITS, YOGURT, PICKLES, FERMENTED FOODS
Salty	ALL TYPES OF SALT, TAMARI, AND SEA VEGETABLES (NORI, DULSE, KOMBU)
Bitter	COFFEE, DARK LEAFY GREENS, AND SPICES (FUNUGREEK, TUMERIC)
Pungent	ONIONS, RADISHES, TURNIPS, AND SPICES (GARLIC, GINGER, MUSTARD SEEDS, ALL KINDS OF PEPPER)
Astringent	CRUCIFEROUS VEGETABLES (BROCCOLI, CAULIFLOWER, CABBAGE), POMEGRANATE, CRANBERRIES, APPLES, PEARS, GREEN TEA, RED WINE, HONEY.

Image 21.3 The Way Food Tastes

The way food acts

The third property of food is the way food acts.

This is the energy that is released after eating it and is either heating or cooling.

To avoid confusion, we are going to focus on spices here. Spices that have the quality of hot are heating, stimulating, and building. They include all types of peppers, cinnamon, fenugreek, mustard seeds, onions, garlic, and ginger. Spices that have the quality of cold are cooling, calming, and breaking down. They include coriander, fennel, cilantro, curry leaf, dill, mint, rose/rose petals, and vanilla. (See image 21.4.)

Heating Stimulating Building	*Cooling Calming Breaking Down*
ASAFOETIDA	CORIANDER
CHILLIES/PEPPER	FENNEL
CINNAMON	CILANTRO
FENUGREEK	CURRY LEAF
MUSTARD/MUSTARD SEED	DILL
ONION	MINT
GARLIC	ROSE/ROSE PETAL
GINGER	VANILLA

Image 21.4 The Way Food Acts

Chapter 22

TOOLS OF YOGA AS REMEDY

Using the tools of yoga as remedy is a simple extension of how they are used to support health, which we have already discussed. Start with breathwork, link it to postures moving dynamically with the inhale and exhale, and focus your mind on a point of attention with a few minutes of meditation.

Please note that the tools of yoga that follow are ones I commonly prescribe; however, they have been organized according to the symptom qualities they *counterbalance* for easier application and use.[15] (See image 22.1.)

---

15. A discussion of the qualities of each specific tool of yoga is beyond the scope of this book.

To COUNTERBALANCE

Air } COLD
LIGHT
DRY
MOBILE

Breath
CALMING
EXTEND EXHALE

Posture
SEATED (LYING)
TWISTING
FORWARD BEND

Meditation
SUN, TREE ROOTS, MOUNTAIN
"I AM CALM."

To COUNTERBALANCE

Fire } HOT
SHARP
OILY
MOBILE

Breath
CALMING
EXTEND EXHALE

Posture
SEATED (LYING)
TWISTING
FORWARD BEND

Meditation
MOON, STILL LAKE
"I AM PEACEFUL."

To COUNTERBALANCE

Earth } STICKY
HEAVY
COLD
STABLE

Breath
ACTIVATING
EXTEND EXHALE

Posture
STANDING
BALANCING
BACKWARD BEND

Meditation
SUN, FIRE, LIGHT
"I AM LIGHT."

Image 22.1 Tools of Yoga as Remedy

Chapter 23

HOW TO COUNTERBALANCE SYMPTOMS

Before I pull everything together, let's review The Counterbalance Solution™, my three-step system to apply the wisdom of Ayurveda for self-healing. The first step is to identify your symptom—physical, mental, or emotional—and its qualities. Next, apply the Golden Principle of "like increases like and opposites reduce" to determine which qualities you need to cultivate to reduce your symptom and support your health. Last, choose the appropriate remedy or remedies that will cultivate the qualities needed. I find that the best way to deepen understanding is to go through examples, so let's review three case studies.

The Counterbalance™ Solution

1 - Identify your symptom (Physical, Mental, or Emotional) and its qualities

2 - Apply the 'Golden Principle.'
   Like increases like.
   Opposites reduce.

3 - Choose remedies to cultivate the <u>opposite</u> qualities.

Case Study #1: Insomnia

(See image 23.1.)

Step 1—Identify your symptom and its qualities.

Insomnia is a symptom with the qualities of air, which are cold, light, dry, and mobile.

Step 2—Apply the Golden Principle.

Using the Golden Principle, "like increases like and opposites reduce," counterbalance and reduce insomnia by cultivating the opposite qualities of hot, heavy, oily, and stable.

Step 3—Choose remedies to cultivate the opposite qualities.

Now we can choose remedies that cultivate these opposite qualities of hot, heavy, oily, and stable.

Routines as remedy.

To cultivate a "grounding" quality of stable, it's important to have an evening and bedtime routine. Many people who have insomnia say that their evenings include lots of "movement"—both physical and mental. They exercise in the evening and then work on their computers after dinner. Instead, it's important to create a feeling of stability to reduce restlessness in the body and mind that is often associated with insomnia. Establishing an evening routine that includes a "tech sabbath" and relaxation will create a feeling of stability. In addition, a regular routine of a cup of tea and self-massage with warm oil (*abhyanga*) before bedtime cultivates the qualities of hot, heavy, and oily.

Diet as remedy.

Let's move on to the second remedy, diet. To cultivate the opposite qualities of hot, heavy, and oily, increase warm, cooked foods prepared in oil and warming spices of ginger and pepper to help decrease insomnia. In addition, replace iced drinks with room temperature or warm water to cultivate the quality of hot.

Tools of yoga as remedy.

The third remedy is the tools of yoga. To cultivate the qualities of heavy and stable, a short, 10-minute practice of some seated yoga poses, exhale-focused breathing, and gratitude meditation as a bedtime routine will help reduce insomnia significantly by pulling the movement of insomnia down to ground it.

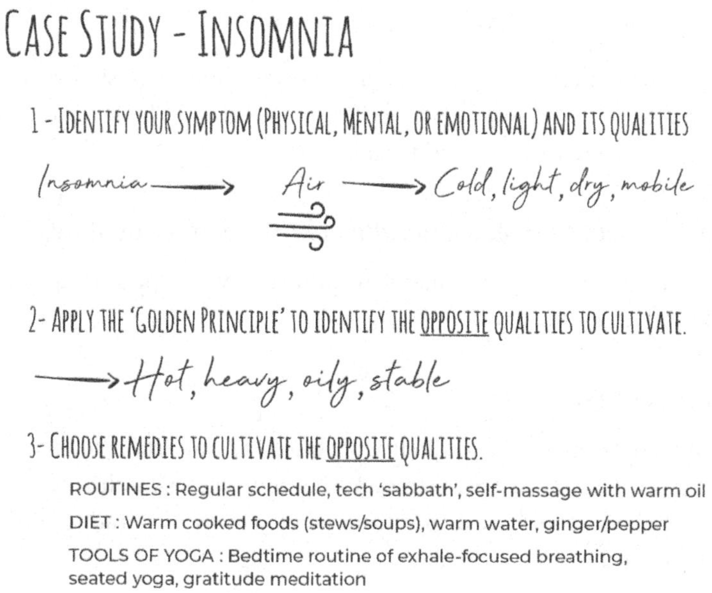

Case Study - Insomnia

1 - Identify your symptom (Physical, Mental, or emotional) and its qualities

Insomnia ——→ *Air* ——→ *Cold, light, dry, mobile*

2 - Apply the 'Golden Principle' to identify the OPPOSITE qualities to cultivate.

——→ *Hot, heavy, oily, stable*

3 - Choose remedies to cultivate the OPPOSITE qualities.

ROUTINES : Regular schedule, tech 'sabbath', self-massage with warm oil

DIET : Warm cooked foods (stews/soups), warm water, ginger/pepper

TOOLS OF YOGA : Bedtime routine of exhale-focused breathing, seated yoga, gratitude meditation

Image 23.1 Case Study—Insomnia

Case Study #2: Acid reflux ("Heartburn")

(See image 23.2.)

Step 1—Identify your symptom and its qualities.

Acid reflux ("heartburn") is a symptom with the qualities of fire, which are hot, sharp, oily, and mobile.

Step 2—Apply the Golden Principle.

Using the Golden Principle, "like increases like and opposites reduce," to counterbalance and reduce acid reflux, we need to cultivate the opposite qualities of cold, dull, dry, and stable.

Step 3—Choose remedies to cultivate the opposite qualities.

Now we can choose remedies that cultivate these opposite qualities of cold, dull, dry, and stable.

Routines as remedy.

To cultivate a "grounding" quality of stable, it's important to have a daily routine, especially with mealtimes. Other routines that cultivate the qualities of light and cold are to add fun and play to the day and to limit time outdoors in the heat of the day.

Diet as remedy.

Many people who have a lot of acid reflux tend to like foods with hot and sharp qualities, such as spicy foods, caffeine, red meat, and alcohol. Avoiding these foods is crucial to help decrease acid reflux. To cultivate the opposite qualities of cold, dull, dry, and stable, increase cooling and dull foods such as vegetables with high water content (cucumbers and melons), as well as cooling spices (cilantro and mint) to help decrease acid reflux.

Tools of yoga as remedy.

To cultivate the qualities of cold and stable, choose slow-paced, restorative, seated, and supine yoga poses that are "grounding" to help reduce acid reflux significantly. Other tools of yoga that cultivate opposite qualities are exhale-focused breathing, gratitude meditation, or meditation upon a visualization of a still lake or the moon.

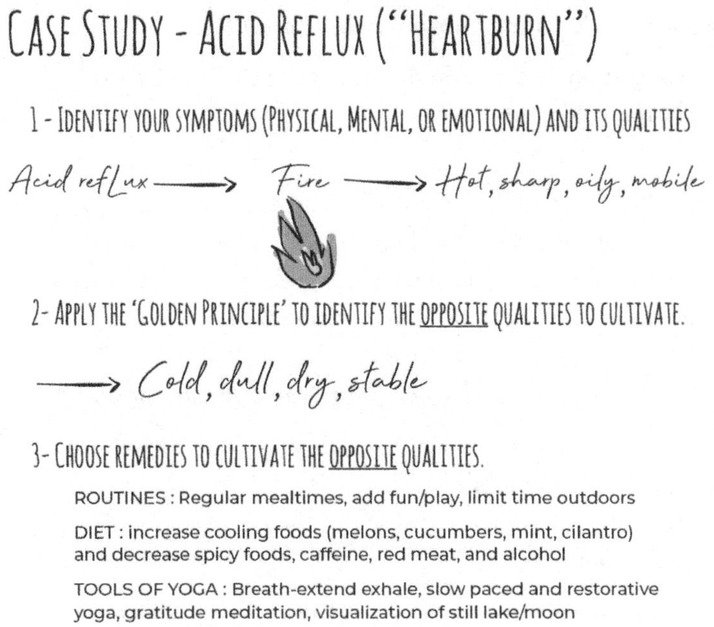

Case Study - Acid Reflux ("Heartburn")

1 - Identify your symptoms (Physical, Mental, or Emotional) and its qualities

Acid reflux ⟶ Fire ⟶ Hot, sharp, oily, mobile

2- Apply the 'Golden Principle' to identify the OPPOSITE qualities to cultivate.

⟶ Cold, dull, dry, stable

3- Choose remedies to cultivate the OPPOSITE qualities.

ROUTINES : Regular mealtimes, add fun/play, limit time outdoors

DIET : increase cooling foods (melons, cucumbers, mint, cilantro) and decrease spicy foods, caffeine, red meat, and alcohol

TOOLS OF YOGA : Breath-extend exhale, slow paced and restorative yoga, gratitude meditation, visualization of still lake/moon

Image 23.2 Case Study—Acid Reflux ("Heartburn")

Case Study #3: Nasal congestion

(See image 23.3.)

Step 1—Identify your symptom and its qualities.

Nasal congestion is a symptom with the qualities of earth, which are sticky, heavy, cold, and stable.

Step 2—Apply the Golden Principle.

Using the Golden Principle, "like increases like and opposites reduce," to counterbalance and reduce nasal congestion, we need to cultivate the opposite qualities of clear, light, hot, and mobile.

Step 3—Choose remedies to cultivate the opposite qualities.

Now we can choose remedies that cultivate these opposite qualities of clear, light, hot, and mobile.

Routines as remedy.

To cultivate movement and the quality of mobile, it's important to keep things moving throughout the body. Waking up earlier in the morning (before 7 a.m.) reduces the collection of mucus caused by sleeping in. In addition, a daily morning practice of nasal cleansing using a neti pot to clear the sinuses and dry brushing the body in the direction of the heart stimulates the movement of lymph.

Diet as remedy.

To cultivate the opposite qualities of clear, light, hot, and mobile in the diet, increase bitter, pungent, and astringent foods such as dark leafy greens, cruciferous vegetables (broccoli, cauliflower, cabbage), onions, radishes, and spices (pepper, garlic, and ginger). In addition, sipping warm water with ginger or a pinch of black pepper throughout the day helps to stimulate digestion and also cultivates the quality of hot.

Tools of yoga as remedy.

To cultivate the qualities of light, hot, and mobile, practice a series of sun salutations or vinyasa yoga. Other tools of yoga that cultivate opposite qualities of hot and mobile are inhale-focused breathing and meditation upon a visualization of the sun, fire, or light.

These case studies show how The Counterbalance Solution™ works, step by step from symptom to remedies, for three common symptoms. However, this system can be applied to any symptom—physical, mental or emotional—giving you the power to self-heal. My hope is that you will use Ayurveda as a health catalyst to create a vibrant life and optimal health.

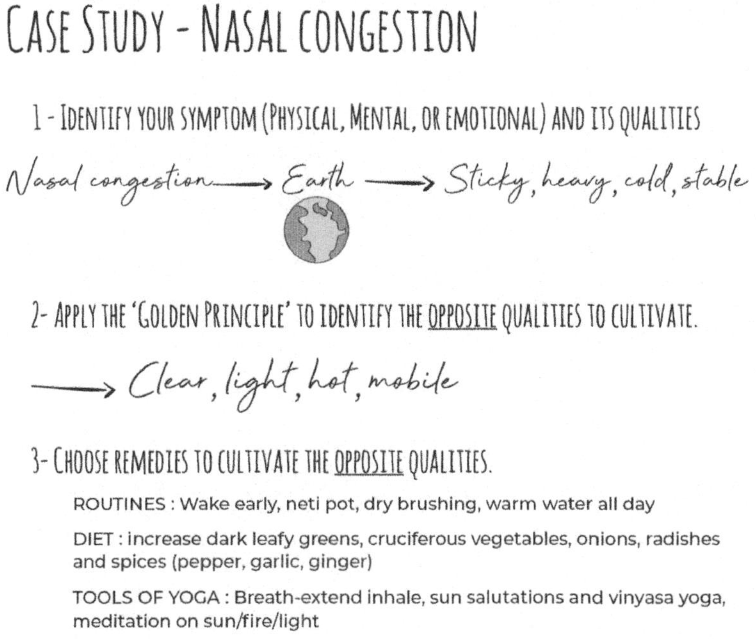

Case Study - Nasal Congestion

1 - Identify your symptom (Physical, Mental, or emotional) and its qualities

Nasal congestion ⟶ Earth ⟶ Sticky, heavy, cold, stable

2- Apply the 'Golden Principle' to identify the OPPOSITE qualities to cultivate.

⟶ Clear, light, hot, mobile

3- Choose remedies to cultivate the OPPOSITE qualities.

ROUTINES : Wake early, neti pot, dry brushing, warm water all day

DIET : increase dark leafy greens, cruciferous vegetables, onions, radishes and spices (pepper, garlic, ginger)

TOOLS OF YOGA : Breath-extend inhale, sun salutations and vinyasa yoga, meditation on sun/fire/light

Image 23.3 Case Study—Nasal Congestion

Chapter 24

CONCLUSION: LIVING AYURVEDA

Of the 4 decades of my life thus far, I have spent half of them studying to become a doctor to help others heal and the other half learning to heal myself by living Ayurveda. Ayurveda has helped me become more mindful of what I do and how I show up in the world. It has helped me live a more meaningful life. For me, Ayurveda is more than just the practice of the principles and the application of the remedies of the ancient medicine of my ancestors. For me, Ayurveda is a return to my roots, a return to my grandfather, a return to my parents and my sister, and a return to my childhood and the dreams I had of one day having the letters "MD" after my name.

And so I've come full circle. From Ayurveda to Western medicine and back to Ayurveda again, I now find myself at the forefront of a "movement that seeks to integrate the best of Western scientific medicine with a broader understanding of the nature of illness, healing and wellness."[16] I now teach hundreds of students and patients about Ayurveda, advocate for yoga therapy in hospitals and collaborate with colleagues to discover innovative ways to bring ancient healing traditions into modern clinical practice.

In recent years, evidence supporting Ayurveda has increased with studies that directly correlate to the healing principles and remedies of Ayurveda. (Even so, whenever I'm asked by my colleagues for evidence that supports Ayurveda, rather than discussing the latest studies, I instead ask them why 5,000 years of evidence isn't sufficient.) In 2017,

---

16. "Integrative Medicine," The Bravewell Collaborative, http://www.bravewell.org/integrative _medicine/

a Nobel Prize was awarded to scientists[17] for their research on circadian medicine, the principles of which can be found in the Ayurvedic clock that details how to live in-sync with nature. Many recent studies on topics such as the healing properties of turmeric and the existence of the "gut-brain" have been published in the most highly regarded medical and scientific journals. These, too, have been known and used for thousands of years in Ayurveda. The tools of yoga are perhaps the most well-studied and well-accepted remedies of Ayurveda at this time in Western medicine. The healing effects of breath, postures, and meditation on practically every system in the human body have become hard to ignore, even for the most skeptical among my medical peers. As a result, the remedies of Ayurveda are emerging from the background, making them common recommendations on the prescription pads of physicians.

But here's the thing. You, dear reader, don't need a prescription from a doctor to access the healing power of this ancient medicine. Instead, you can use what you've learned in this book to write your own prescription for self-healing through Ayurveda.

All you have to do is listen—because the healer lies within.

AVANTI KUMAR SINGH

---

17.   Jeffrey C. Hall, Michael Rosbash, and Michael W. Young

RESOURCES

Living Ayurveda

1 APPLY THE COUNTERBALANCE™ SOLUTION
- IDENTIFY THE QUALITIES OF THE SYMPTOM.
- APPLY "THE GOLDEN PRINCIPLE."
- CHOOSE REMEDIES TO CULTIVATE OPPOSITE QUALITIES.

2 CONSIDER YOUR DAILY ROUTINES.

3 LINK AND LAYER ROUTINES AS REMEDY.

4 LINK AND LAYER DIET AS REMEDY.

5 LINK AND LAYER TOOLS OF YOGA AS REMEDY.

Daily Routine for Self-Healing

- Wake with the sun (by 6AM)
- Drink a glass of warm water with lemon upon waking
- Rinse your eyes, mouth/tongue to remove impurities accumulated overnight
- Evacuate bowels as early in the motning as possible
- Move to get moving with 10 minutes of gentle yoga or stretching
- Eat an early, light, and easy-to-digest breakfast

- Sip warm water all day long
- Eat your largest and main meal of the day at lunch - between noon and 2-PM
- Go for a walk and take 1,000 Steps
- Take pauses throughout the day for 5 seconds and breathe gently
- Create a quiet buffer-zone of 15 minutes to transition from work to home

- Eat dinner early (by 7-8 PM)
- Turn off electronics by 8PM
- Promote healthy sleep with an evening practice (tea, bath)
- Massage your feet
- Sleep by 10 PM

GLOSSARY OF AYURVEDIC TERMS

Abhyanga—self-massage with warm oil

Agni—digestive fire

Ama—accumulated toxins (waste) that have not been digested, absorbed, or eliminated; toxic load

Asana—a steady and comfortable posture; a tool of yoga

Ayurveda—the "science of life"; traditional healing science of India

Bhavana—visualization; a tool of yoga

Dhyana—meditation, a technique to merge the mind with a point of attention, to cultivate a state of inward awareness; a tool of yoga

Dinacharya—daily routine

Dosha—a mind-body constitution, energy; the five elements are combined to create the three doshas

Guna—a quality; 20 qualities that describe everything in nature that are organized into 10 pairs

Kapha—one of the three doshas, the mind-body constitution of earth and water; the main qualities are cold, sticky, heavy, and stable

Kitchari—a cleansing food made of split mung beans, white basmati rice, and healing spices

Mahabhuta—an element, of which there are five: air, space, fire, water, and earth

Mantra—sound or affirmation; a tool of yoga

Mudra—gesture; a tool of yoga

Ojas—vitality that creates strength, immunity, and longevity

Pitta—one of the three doshas, the mind-body constitution of fire and water; the main qualities are hot, sharp, oily, and mobile

Prakruti—one's genetic blueprint or given nature that is established upon conception; a state of balance

Prana—vital life force energy that is essential for existence

Pranayama—breathwork, a technique that breaks unconscious patterns and causes many changes in the physiology of the body and the mind; a tool of yoga

Ritucharya—seasonal routine

Vata—one of the three doshas, the mind-body constitution of air and space; the main qualities are cold, light, dry, and mobile

Vikruti—nurture, a state of imbalance from one's genetic blueprint/given nature

Yoga—sister science of Ayurveda, which has many tools

ACKNOWLEDGMENTS

I am grateful to many people without whom this book never would have been written. Their love, support, and encouragement kept me going through a process that was much harder than I expected and even more rewarding than I imagined.

Thank you, Amy Wheeler, Indu Arora, Laura Jane Murphy, Nancy Heap, Pratima Raichur, and Melinda Ring—my teachers, mentors, and wise women who believed that I had something important to share with the world. You not only generously shared your knowledge with me but also shared your classrooms, studios, and stages with me so that I could teach what eventually would become the basis for this book.

To Alexia Vernon, Bhavena Taneja, Cheena Chandra, Elizabeth Shaw, Harleen Singh, Heather Gunther, Jaslyn Singh, Jessica Lederhausen, Jill Castle, Jill Glavan, Julie Stewart, Lori Waterstraat, Malika Ameen, Meredith Harbour, Rachna Narula, Richa Pal, Ruby Singh, Shummi Singh, and Tanmeet Sethi—my circle of amazing women who held a vision for me of what this book could be. Over the past 2 years, you reminded me of that vision with phone calls and text messages, during mastermind sessions and meditations, and over coffee and cocktails. You inspire me every day with the healing work you are doing in the world. I am so grateful to each of you.

To Azul Terronez. You truly are the "book whisperer" and always kept me focused on just the next step so I could hand in my final manuscript in less than a year. Thank you for helping bring my stories to life and for helping me turn my idea into this book. I could not have finished this without your keen insight and guidance.

Thank you, Mummy and Papa, for always believing in me when I didn't believe in myself. You are the reason I am who I am today.

To Anjali, my little sister, who is my biggest champion. Thank you for being the coolest, the funniest, and the most free-spirited and adventurous human I know. You may be younger than I am, but I look up to you—you know how to suck the marrow out of life.

To Zayn and Isha, the two halves of my heart. Thank you for choosing me to guide you in this lifetime . . . although the truth is that you both are my greatest teachers. I love you more than you will ever know.

To Kanwar, my partner in everything. Thank you for showing me what love is and reminding me every day that the purpose of life is to live a life of purpose. I am so proud of the legacy we are creating together.

And to every patient and student who has come to learn from me, thank you for the great honor of being one of many guides on your healing journey. You inspire me to continue to aspire to be of greater service to the world.

ABOUT THE AUTHOR

Avanti Kumar-Singh is a physician who, after extensive medical training, began a journey to find her joy again—and to help people truly heal. Realizing that "you can quit your job, but you can't quit your calling," Avanti set out to discover what really makes people healthy and what predisposes them to illness. She is now on a mission to evolve the conversation and to create a movement in which medical professionals reclaim the "art" of medicine and become heart-centered, healing catalysts who practice true medicine and support self-healing in their patients.

Through a powerful mix of expert knowledge and communication, Avanti serves as a catalyst for transformation toward more vitality and, ultimately, more joy in everyone she works with. Her courses, writings, and lectures beautifully bridge the gap between the technological advances of Western medicine and the traditional, equally effective practices of Eastern medicine. Avanti is a portal to demystifying and understanding the power and beauty of Ayurveda.

Over the 20 years of her training, study, and research, Avanti has shared her expertise with Fortune 500 companies, at elite undergraduate and graduate institutions, and at prestigious industry and medical conferences. She has also been featured in the Huffington Post, Thrive Global,

Well + Good, goop, and mindbodygreen and served as the co-lead facilitator of the Faculty Scholars Program in Integrative Healthcare at the OSHER Center for Integrative Medicine at Northwestern Medicine. She is a sought-after speaker and the host of the top-rated health and wellness podcast "The Healing Catalyst." Dr. Avanti currently serves as the Director of Ayurveda at BIÂN Chicago.

Avanti holds a BA in art history from the University of Chicago and an MD from Rush University College of Medicine. She is also a certified plant-based professional and a certified yoga therapist. Avanti lives in Chicago with her husband and two children. *The Health Catalyst* is her first book.

Web: avantikumarsingh.com
Instagram: @avantikumarsingh
Podcast: The Healing Catalyst

If you enjoyed this book and
found it helpful, please
leave a **REVIEW** on Amazon.

Visit me at

AVANTIKUMARSINGH.COM

where you can find more resources
and sign up for email updates.

Thank You!

Made in the USA
Coppell, TX
17 October 2022

84812014R00095